CHRISTOPHER LOGUE'S

Bumper Book of

TRUE STORIES

Drawings by Bert Kitchen

PRIVATE EYE

Published in Great Britain 1980 by
Private Eye Productions Limited,
34 Greek Street, London W1.
In association with Andre Deutsch Limited,
105 Great Russell Street, London WC1.

Drawings copyright Bert Kitchen

Pressdram Limited.
ISBN 233 97305 2

Designed by Donald Macpherson
Printed in Great Britain by Halstan & Co.,
Amersham, Bucks.

O.H.M.S.nail

Mrs Doris Honeysett received a tattered and grubby letter accompanied by a note from the Post Office explaining that it had been eaten by snails.
Daily Mirror, 19.10.70

In 1961 I received a letter from Andrew Osmond asking me if I would like to write for *Private Eye.*

Having already collected what seemed to be a large number of absurd or pathetic news items, I rewrote and submitted half-a-dozen of them as *True Stories* — a title taken from the romantic magazine.

As my copy was liked I continued as I had begun and, after four or five issues of *Private Eye, True Stories* had the makings of a regular feature. But this was uncertain until, my collection being almost exhausted, Richard Ingrams invited the magazine's readers to become, by clipping and sending in stories they thought suitable, the column's "monitors".

Since then I have received about 40 stories a fortnight, getting on for 20,000 all told, from, at a guess, some 15,000 people.

Generally, because I do not check their source, I alter the names of the people and sometimes of the location in the stories I use. If the provenance of a story is missing in this collection it is because after a year I throw away the clippings on which the story was based, and, when the copy for an issue of *Private Eye* has been composed and laid out, the story Bert Kitchen has chosen to illustrate is placed at the head of the column: therefore the information at the column's foot no longer tallies with the sequence of stories as published.

Nevertheless, though I may have added a year or two to this gentleman's age, or a word or two to that lady's statement, of the stories I have rewritten for *Private Eye*, one, and only one, has been bogus.

Not long ago a series of articles about do-it-yourself home conversions appeared in a Sunday colour supplement. The issue of the newspaper that followed the issue of its supplement that described the difference between the retaining and the dividing walls of a house included an apology, saying: what was shown as a typical dividing wall on page so-and-so of our last colour supplement was, in fact, a typical retaining wall, and vice-versa.

I invented a couple who, having followed the false distinction, brought down their home about their ears.

I would like to thank the members of the human and the animal kingdoms who did and said what subsequently was literalized, the reporters who traipsed round, the monitors who clipped, and the editor and the staff of *Private Eye* who saw the stories into print again.

Christopher Logue

AFRICA

What Comes First?

A South African hen living on a farm near Oudtshoorn laid an egg weighing 16 ounces, climbed out of its nest and dropped dead.
Evening Standard

Handy Solution

When Mr Jeliud Mayo of Kericho, Kenya, found that his mother had failed to add any meat to his stew, he cut off her hand and threw it into the pot.

Mr L.B. Auma, Senior Resident Magistrate of Kericho, said that Mr Mayo's action was "very inconsiderate".
Daily Nation, 28.2.75

Fisherman's Bait

During his trial for molesting a wild animal in the Kreuger National Park, Eastern Transvaal, Mr Petrus Johannes Shitkoff said:

"I had been driving about the park for nine days without seeing a single animal. Suddenly I saw a family of lions eating their kill; I became very excited, forgot myself and pelted them with oranges from the window of my car."

Mr Rundt, defending, said: "Mr Shitkoff is president of a Cape angling club. It was he who taught Dr Verwoerd to fish."

He was fined £200.
The Times

Heart Trouble

*Mr George Least, a dairyman
from Salisbury, Rhodesia, who
had recently been given a
second heart to back up his
own, shot himself for love of a
nurse he met while recovering
from the operation.*
Daily Mirror, 15.11.77

Black Beestes

A white South African walked into a swarm of
bees. Their stings turned him black.

The sufferer had to await the call of a "black"
ambulance, suffer the humiliation of a "black"
hospital ward, and undergo the considerable
danger of a delay in treatment when the medical
authorities found out that he was "white" and
insisted on his being transferred to a "white"
hospital ward.

His condition remains critical. However, if he
dies, he will have the satisfaction of knowing that
principle was supported to the end.

Dr Carel de Wet, Minister of Health, said:
"Apartheid does not apply in medical emergencies."
Daily Telegraph, 17.1.70

AMERICA

Bad News

Sixteen months after the first of its bi-weekly issues, an American newspaper whose editorial policy was to print no news save good news closed down.

Called Good News, published from Sacramento, and with a circulation in all 50 of the United States, the paper did not announce its own failure.

"Such an item would have been against our policy," said its founder Mr William Bailey — father of twelve.

The last issue of Good News contained the following headlines: "196,459,483 citizens were not killed in auto accidents this year"; "Fantastic drop in suicide rate"; "No war declared in sixteen weeks"; "Triple rapist enters monastery".
Evening Standard, 8.4.72

Gift Rap

A long line of children were waiting to be photographed with Santa Claus in the Monterey Park Shopping Center, California.

A young woman jumped the queue and said to the traditionally dressed Santa: "Three lids, please."

"That will be $30.00," said Santa. "The stuff is in my toybag."

Whereupon the young woman revealed herself as an undercover FBI agent and arrested Santa for dealing in marijuana.

He went quietly, accompanied by the screams of the queue.
Herald Tribune, 20.12.71

Screen Idolatry

After giving a lecture explaining why the US space scientists had to spend £7,140 million per annum, Dr Werner Von Braun said he was prepared to answer questions. The first came from an elderly lady who asked:

"Why don't we just stay at home and watch television as God intended?"
Anon

Counter Feat

Mrs Marva Dew, a 91-year-old chiropractor of Waterloo, Iowa, completed a book which she described as "experimental", the text of which had been composed by her typing out every number from 1 to 1,000,000.

"It took me five years and over 60 reams of paper to defeat the challenge," she said.

"One day a regular patient of mine said that nobody could count up to a million. He was wrong."
San Francisco Chronicle, 10.12.74

Bare Bounty

The day after he inherited £20,000,000, Mr Stuart Holzman of Fort Lauderdale, Florida, drove a new speedboat with a cargo of four nude playmates among the pleasure craft anchored in Bimimi marina.

Two of the playmates held a large satchel filled with 100-dollar bills which the other two scattered along the water.

"My uncle insisted on my having a responsible job until I was thirty-five," he said, "and for fifteen years I have been a rodent officer. Yesterday was my 35th birthday and I hope I shall never have to be responsible again."

Four pleasure-lovers were drowned in their attempts to fish for the money.

Kayham International, 26.5.73

Thanks a Million

The acquisition of wealth preoccupied Mr O. Nelms throughout his lifetime. In the early days he gave away cigars upon whose bands the slogan "Help O. Nelms make a million dollars" was inscribed. Reaching this figure, he placed an advertisement in his local paper, saying: "Thanks for helping O. Nelms make his million", which advertisement he repeated each year for 24 years, amending the final words of his message to "another million".

Recently O. Nelms died. His will settled $9,000,000.00 in a Trust Fund whose sole purpose is to arrange an annual cocktail party for the citizens of Dallas, the town that supported his campaign. The centrepiece of these occasions will be Mr Nelms' hermetically sealed coffin, through whose small window the guests will be able to toast the object of their generosity.
Daily Telegraph

Well, I Declare

During a New York-Miami jet flight Mr Justin McDonough, the actor, decided to learn his lines. On landing he was surprised to be the only one who stood up, and shocked when several heavily armed policemen entered the plane and arrested him to the Stewardess's cry of "That's the one!".

Overhearing Mr McDonough's mutter, a female passenger told the Stewardess who told the Pilot who told Ground Control Miami that a revolutionary hijacker was aboard, "talking to himself about slavery, freedom, and the necessity of overthrowing bad government".

After showing the police his script, Mr McDonough was released.

He had been learning the Declaration of Independence.
Evening Standard, 16.4.69

Mad Luck!

Having concealed himself in a redundant ice-box, Dr R.H. Hales, a 53-year-old criminal psychopath from 'Byeways' (Indiana State's biggest lunatic asylum) escaped and, two days later, presented himself to the Appointments Board of 'White-hill' (Indiana State's biggest penitentiary) as a potential Senior Medical Advisor.

"Dr Hales gave a brilliant interview," said Mrs Waram Fulger, the Appointment Board's Chairman. "We gave him the job at a salary of $35,000 a year."

Dr Hales remained in his position until his photograph appeared in a local paper.
Daily Mail, 16.7.75

Apart From That, Mr Rieske. . .

Mr W.M. Rieske of Salt Lake City, Utah, built a 16-foot-high, fully articulated effigy of Abraham Lincoln, installed with a tape-deck that, at a given signal, reproduced the 16th President's greatest speeches through the effigy's lips.

Some 3,000 citizens gathered at the Northgate Shopping Center, Seattle, for the first performance. Mr Rieske pressed the starting button and the electric Abraham began.

Hardly were the words "What is that we hold most dear amongst us?" out of its mouth than the effigy abandoned its dignified gestures and, twisting itself into a spasm-racked pretzel, sang:

I wanna yell, pretty momma,
I wanna get my rocks joy
free,
I wanna feel that love pain,
momma,
I wanna rock you close to
me. . .

"It was a harmonics problem," said Mr Rieske. "The local rock station swamped our circuitry with a more powerful signal."
Evening Standard, 8.1.73

Kinetic Justice

During a ceremony at the Kemper Arena, Kansas City, at which the building's designer, Mr Helmut Jahn, was to receive a citation from the president of the American Institute of Architects, watched by 1,000 of the Institute's members, the roof of the $12 million building fell in. Twenty-six architects were hospitalised.

The Architects' Journal, 18.7.79

Bottom Bid

At a West Coast auction a Hollywood antiquarian outbid all comers for a lavatory seat used by Herr Adolf Hitler.

Sun, 19.12.69

THE ARTS

Royal Dressing-down

After visiting a local art gallery, Councillor Wood of Sunderland felt obliged to issue a protest.

The objects that excited him were life-size figures of the Royal Family dressed entirely in rags.

"The vast majority of people", said Councillor Wood, "would find these figures offensive. They are dressed in tatters. They look like tramps."

The sculptor, Mr J. Bulmer of Stocksfield, aged 93, said: "I am an ardent royalist but my pension doesn't run to a lot of fancy clothing."
Daily Mail, 21.5.74

Prize Fight

Invited to attend an arts festival devoted to singing and dancing, the ochre-daubed warriors of Okapa, New Guinea, were so surprised when the judges failed to award them the first prize that they shot arrows into the audience of jet tourists.

Without more ado the attendants, who were riot police in disguise, charged the stone-age tribesmen. The Okapa warriors stood their ground. It was not until the tourists joined forces with the police that the performers were overwhelmed and chased back into the jungle.
Evening Standard, 27.4.72

Plucky Performance

An audience of well-heeled theatre-lovers attending an open-air charity performance of A Midsummer Night's Dream were roused from their torpor when a man dressed as a chicken leapt onto the stage, flapped his wings and cried "ORK!"

Speaking from the dock, Mr I.S. Hinchcliffe said: "I had been wandering about the countryside for several hours looking for a fancy dress ball promised by invitation. I thought I had arrived at last."

Mr Herbert O'Dell, presiding, said: "We don't like this sort of thing in Woburn. The maximum fine is £10. I fine you £10."

Bedford Record, 31.7.73

Back Pack

During a hearing by the State Supreme Court of an application to ban the practice of tattooing, authorities from the New York Health Department maintained that the tattooing habit was not confined to the lower classes.

As evidence, they stated that Lady Randolph Churchill and Alfonso XII of Spain had both been liberally tattooed. General Montgomery was alleged to have had pink rats dancing across his belly, and an unnamed Admiral of The Fleet was said to have had a complete hunt with horses, dogs and men emblazoned in full cry down his back, all chasing a fox, whose tail could be seen disappearing into the only burrow.
New Scientist

The Last Supper

Over 300 people arrived at the Barmera theatre near Adelaide for a *show-banquet*. During a performance of a play called *The Bard's Banquet* the audience would receive a five-course dinner, each course to be served at the same time as a similar course was carried onstage for the actors.

The Bard's Banquet is set in the Mermaid Tavern. The action consists of Messrs Jonson, Shakespeare, Marlowe et al eating a huge meal, singing various popular songs, and telling stories about their lives.

Because the food for the audience was late, the curtain did not go up until 10.30 pm — "by which time", said Mr Robin Williams, the front-of-house manager, "most of the audience were hungry and drunk.

"As the actors consumed their first course (potted shrimps), several people of both sexes began to shout out that the food should be divided between cast and audience. And when Mr Bee (who was playing the part of Shakespeare) appealed for order he was pelted with beer cans.

"By the time the roast ox was carried on," Mr Williams continued, "the audience had lost control. A man jumped onto the stage and began to throw portions of the ox into the auditorium. Then some of the crowd occupied the stage, threw the actors into the stalls, and fought hand-to-hand battles with those who had not managed to get so much as a piece of bread.

"One couple, shouting out 'We don't care! We don't care!' began to make love in the middle of the fight; and, as the police had to drive 50 miles to reach the scene, nobody stopped them."

Mr John Voysey, an official of the Arts Council of South Australia (which sponsored the event) said: "It was a nightmare happening before my eyes. These people do not know what art is. I think Barmera should be bombed flat."

The Melbourne Age, 8.8.78

The Slings and Arrows. . .

A production of *Hamlet* by the Keswick Polytechnic included many changes. The text was cut to 15 minutes, "because there are several other things on the bill", and retitled *Hamlette*, "because we could only get two male actors," said Miss Joanna Ripe, the director/adaptor.

"The whole thing is set in a nunnery," she said. "We gave Claudia — Hamlette's aunt — most of Polonius' lines, because she learnt his part by mistake."

Miss Ripe added several new parts to the play — Joyce, Hamlette's sister and friend; Dinah, a blackamoor, whose part was made up of lines taken from the Nurse in *Romeo and Juliet*, "with the dirt removed", and Louise, a girl disguised as a male deaf-mute, who drowns herself out of pique.
North Circular, Vol. 7 No. 1

Breast Plates

Members of the Welsh Arts Council Sculpture Committee attended a luncheon at which food was dished up onto a service created by sculptress Beryl Cheame from mouldings of her own body.

"My breasts did for the soup bowls and my tummy for the plates," she said. "Later I added a casserole which was formed around a cast of my behind.

"I do not feel the least embarrassed by having people eat off my body — so to speak. I am completely detached.

"I got the idea during a dinner party. All at once I realised what a marvellous food container the body is."
The People, 30.7.74

Cannon Balls-up

Intending to mark his appointment as conductor of the Atlanta Symphony Orchestra by an unusual performance, Mr Robert Shaw installed 16 electronically fired mini-cannon throughout the auditorium.

Halfway through the *1812 Overture* he pressed the button marked 'Fire Cannon One', whereupon all 16 fired together, stunning the 15,000-strong audience and filling the great dome with smoke.

Hardly had the music lovers staggered to their feet when the Smell-All-Tell-All Customer Safety System drenched them with anti-burn foam.

While recovering in the foyer the strongest and luckiest members of the audience were brutally thrust aside by over 50 members of the Atlanta Emergency Fire-Fighting Crew, who charged into the orchestra pit with cries of "Geronimo!".

"I have to admit to a number of incidents," said Fire Captain Bronski. "The fighters were wearing a new model of smoke-mask and some of them could not see."
Daily Telegraph, 28.6.74

Raise You. . .

Complaints laid by the Reverend Donald Pattison of Chelmsford obliged the town's Art Festival Committee to withdraw a painting from their exhibition.

The painting showed Christ playing poker with friends.

"I am quite sure Christ did not play cards," said the Reverend Pattison, "and certainly not after rising from the dead."
South London Press, 3.9.71

Explicit Hex

Written on the door of a lavatory in the railway station at Bognor Regis:

"I would like to get hold of a Rocker with blond hair and say to him I am going to put you into a bath of cold water and hold your head under the water and bring your head up again and comb your nice blond hair and say to you now I am going to drown you. Now the Rocker will scream for help but I will hold the Rocker under to drown. Drown all Rockers. I am a Mod."

Anon

Bird Brained

Receiving a Christmas card from her friend Mrs Massingham, Mrs Wright neglected to read the verse until her grand-daughter asked her the meaning of the stanza's penultimate word.

Told to read it aloud, the child began:

"A robin redbreast on my sill
Sang for a crust of bread.
I slowly brought the window down
And smashed his fucking head."

"I do not think this sort of card should be sold at Christmas time," said Mrs Wright.

A spokesman from the Greeting Card Association said: "This verse is about 120 years old and is well-known to card collectors."

Daily Mirror, 4.2.69

BROADCASTING

Dimblebore

Mr James Mulungushi, the "Richard Dimbleby of Zambia", was reprimanded for accompanying a broadcast of President Kaunda's vanishing motorcade with the words: "And I return you to the studio as the President goes slowly round the bend."
Salisbury Herald

Recorded Live

Overcome by despair, Mr Thomas Helms, a painter, threw himself off the 86th floor of the Empire State Building in New York, but was blown by a gust of wind into the studios of the NBC television company three floors down during a broadcast of 'How Are You Now?', a This Is Your Life-type bio-slot.

Put straight on camera and interviewed about his decision, Mr Helms said that he had changed his mind soon after he left the parapet.
Daily Telegraph, 9.1.78

Gift from God

Viewers of the 'A Few Minutes With God' television programme — part of the Christmas Evening Hour on Melbourne's Channel 7 — were surprised when a sermon on Decency In The Home by the Rev. Sydney Corker was interrupted by a clip from a pornographic film.

"It was a tri-state, on-, in-, and outgoing satellite Telcon screening," said the Station Manager, Yvonne Maguire. "But I suspect local interference because the clip, which showed a hockey team getting together with the members of a well-known Melbourne golfing club was the same one as we had at out office party last week."

Informed that the viewing figures for his programme had leapt by over 2000% in 35 seconds, Rev. Corker said: "This is unusual."

Courier Mail, 27.12.79

Unofficial Receiver

Shortly after visiting her dentist a housewife of Daytona Beach, Florida, was awakened in the middle of the night by her husband who complained that her teeth were broadcasting. He was right.

Her dentist, Dr John Long, explained that certain metallic fillings can create a receiving set when contacted by acidulous saliva.

"It will pass off in a few days," he said. "Meantime, keep your mouth closed as much as you can, for its natural cavity forms an effective baffle box, thereby increasing the volume."

The lady did as she was told and the broadcasts ceased. "I thought I was free of the trouble and ready to throw a party," she said. "But no sooner were things under way than I opened my mouth to laugh and out came the theme song from *Doctor Zhivago*, followed by *Rambling Rose*. Fortunately our friends are all broadminded. Some of them even danced to the tunes."

Ottawa Journal, 9.4.70

BUSINESS

Stacked with Interest

A man walked into an Esher bank and asked to speak to the manager. Shown into that gentleman's office, he asked if he might have a loan.

When the manager heard that his visitor was not one of the bank's clients, he explained that loans were made only to customers with accounts. Why not open one?

"But I only want £2," said the man, "in return for which I am prepared to offer my car as security."

Having examined the car the manager agreed to the loan although, as he pointed out, the proceedings were slightly unusual.

The stranger left and the car was placed in the bank's garage.

Two months later, the customer entered the bank and asked for the return of his car, giving the manager the £2 borrowed. The manager pointed out that there was interest to pay: the sum of fourpence. This the customer paid. As he was leaving, the manager asked why he had wanted to borrow only two pounds.

"Where else can I garage my car for two months for fourpence?" said the man.

Anon

Sex Crazed

Interviewed after she had been arrested for shoplifting, Miss Yvonne Bullen, the sex star and owner of a chain of sex stores, said: "I just did not know what I was doing. It has been nothing but work, work, work for the last two years. In over 30 sex films I have performed more than 2,000 erotico-gymnastic acts. You can see that I am dazed by it all because the goods for which I forgot to pay were all dog-foods and I poisoned my alsatian Casanova by mistake last week."

Miss Bullen said that she planned to give up her acting and become an undertaker.
Sunday Mirror, 12.8.78

Sackcloth & Clashes

"Although we had been separated for over 30 years I was shocked by the manner in which the Rumshaw Funeral Service treated poor Tom's remains," said Mrs Joan Barton of Leeds.

"When I arrived at his house I had no idea that the two-tone estate car with its tail-gate up was Rumshaw's new-style hearse.

"I was about to speak to the young man in a cap who was standing about on the lawn when the first-floor window opened and a large sack was pushed out. The young man made an effort to catch it but the weight was too much for him.

"Then another, much older man appeared from inside the house and helped his friend to dump the sack into the estate car. Only when they were about to drive away did I discover that the sack contained Tom."

"People are very difficult to please nowadays," said Mr Frederick Main, a director of Rumshaw's. "Both persons mentioned by the complainant are holders of the Inter-ment Diploma and are members of the National Association of Embalmers and Taxidermists. We use the bag if the stair-case is difficult to negotiate. It is very difficult to attract young people towards the profession. They do not like to be seen in hearses or wearing top-hats, so we use happy-type vehicles and wear jeans."
Anon

Naked Absurdity

A company director, Mr Paul Malzarede, has been fined £150 for dictating letters to his secretary in the nude.

The incident would not have become a case had the seventy-year-old director resisted the temptation to fire his pistol at an imaginary burglar during a power cut.
Birmingham Evening Mail, 19.12.69

Royal Warranty

Having acquired a twenty-foot-high fibreglass statue of King Kong, Mr Pacey, a secondhand-car dealer of Camp Hill, Coventry, renamed his firm The King Kong Kar Kompany.

Within hours of opening his new concern Mr Pacey received a letter from the Business Names section of the Department of Trade and Industry forbidding him to use the term King Kong "as it implies Royal patronage".

"I shall complain to the Queen," said Mr Pacey. "There was not the slightest risk of confusion. At the time I had him dressed up as Santa Claus."
Grapevine, '73-'74

Sticky Problem

*Having issued a stamp sur-
charged YAHWEH, the Israeli
government were obliged to
withdraw it. Licking God's
name is forbidden. By the
same token, the stamps
cannot be destroyed. Sealed
vaults were filled at the behest
of the superstitious.*
Guardian, 11.11.70

Sago Sages

Mr Djambi and Mr Hasnuddin of Haruku, Indo-
nesia, both laid claims to the same sago tree. As
property lovers and strong traditionalists, they
decided to settle the matter in the time-honoured
way — by seeing who could remain underwater
the longer.

Watched by their fellow villagers, the rivals
weighted themselves with stones and jumped into
the sea.

Both drowned.
Birmingham Evening Mail, 22.10.70

Chef d'Oeuvre

A £100 limited edition of
The Rhyme Of The Ancient
Mariner *has been published by
Mrs Josie Holton.*

*Restricted to 100 copies,
the poem is printed on
seven varieties of seaweed.
"This is my first attempt to
produce a book printed on
seaweed," said Mrs Holton. "I
used edible seaweeds only. If
you get fed up with the book
you can always eat it."*
Daily Express, 5.5.72

Stormy Petrol

*An executive from one of the oil companies was detailed
to watch the behaviour of potential customers when faced
with self-serving petrol machines.*

*One lady arrived, got out of her car, read the instruct-
ions and inserted a £1 note down the nozzle of the hose.
Finding that nothing came of this, she shouted: "Five
gallons of regular, you twit!" down the same nozzle. After
that she left in a bad temper.*

*She was followed by a man who wrote his name and
address on a piece of paper and popped it into the slot
designed to take £1 notes. Asked why he was doing this,
he said: "It said 'Insert a note', so I did."*
Sun, 13.8.71

O.H.M.S.nail

Mrs Doris Honeysett
received a tattered and grubby
letter accompanied by a note
from the Post Office explaining
that it had been eaten by
snails.
Daily Mirror, 19.10.70

Close of Trading

The body of a man dressed in a pin-stripe suit with an umbrella under his arm was found sitting in a crevice halfway down a cliff near Land's End. He was facing out to sea.
Guardian, 16.2.70

Gift Suggestion

As a promotional incentive, a firm of Californian undertakers offered a £200 free funeral to those who die on Christmas Day.
Southern Evening Echo, 20.12.69

Games People Play

"Just to show that our organisation is unstuffy," said Mrs Worplow of the Weybridge Marriage Guidance Service, "we invited Sheikh Zotan who owns the local sex shop to perform at our fete. He was lovely. He stuck a pin through his neck, ate fire, and allowed our Chairman to smash open a concrete brick that he balanced on his head."

Interviewed at his home, Sheikh Zotan (Mr Seymour Tuffin) said: "Although we are competitors, so to speak, I had to do it as they are a charity. I see a lot more of marriage guidance problems than they do."
News & Advertiser, 17.8.79

Imperial Measure

Mr Robert Pierpoint, a Red Cross official, explained that the shipment of many thousand brassieres as part of the famine relief to East Pakistan was not entirely useless.

"We used the cups to measure out rations of flour to the starving," he said.

Anon

Amelia de la Lune

Called to a good-news interview, Mr & Mrs John Fallsoft were delighted to hear that a distant cousin of Mrs Sue Fallsoft, Miss Amelia McCaby of Euston, Vermont, had left them £400,000.

Miss McCaby's only stipulation was that, before they got the money, they had to see that she was buried on the moon.

Anon

A Touch of Brass

The Journal of the American Library Association announced the publication of *Playboy* magazine in a Braille edition.

Stoke Evening Sentinel, 16.4.71

That's Odd!

Mr Roger Beamish, the manager of a South Coast shoe shop, was disappointed when his free offer of a selection of odd shoes to local one-legged men failed to produce a significant response.

"Our customers are constantly making off with odd shoes," he said. "The only person who took us up on the offer was a Mr Michael Nipper, who plays Long John Silver in Plymouth's granddad punk group, The Unhappy Pirates."

Daily Mail, January 1978

CHURCH TIMES

Joke Butty

Forty members of Calderbrook's Mothers' Union boarded a coach for their annual outing. The trip was a visit to the best fish and chip shop in England, allegedly in Guisley, Yorkshire.

Gentlemen are banned from this outing.

The ladies were barely on their way when some of them noticed a strange woman on the back seat. She was dressed in a mini-skirt, tartan stockings, large plastic earrings, and had a clean band of eyeshadow on each lid.

When the group arrived at the chippery, they were surprised to see the young woman hitch up her tiny skirt and take her money out of her drawers.

They questioned her about this and discovered that the stranger was the Rev. Francis Brumwell, dressed in drag.

"I wore my wife's clothes," he said. "On the way home they all called me Celia."

Anon

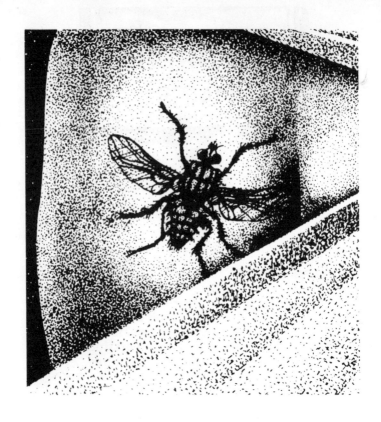

God's Little Creature

An unknown man who claimed to be God was knocked down and killed by a heavy tractor in Mt Bruno, Canada.

"I was selling flowers at the corner of Naysmith Square," said Mrs Barbara Eastman, "when this man came up and said 'I am God — could you direct me to the nearest church, please?' When I had given him the proper directions he took off his hat, said 'Thank you', stepped out into the road and was instantly killed by the tractor."

A spokesman for the Mounted Police said: "The only distinguishing mark was a tattoo of a fly on the man's left buttock."

Toronto Globe & Mail, 4.10.78

Battle Hymns

In order to compete for the Golden Harp, a religious trophy awarded on a triennial basis, 30 provincial choirs assembled and performed before the judge, Reverend Father de Liss, in Lusaka Cathedral.

After the final round, sung between the Kimbu and Dara village choirs, the Rev. de Liss announced that Kimbu Choir's rendering of "Good Shepherd, lead Thy peaceful flock" had been surpassed by no more than a hair during Dara Choir's version of "Love Thy neighbour, love Thy Lord".

This decision was unpopular.

Inspector Empibo of Lusaka said: "By the time we reached the Cathedral both choirs were involved in a pitched battle.

"The choirboys, average age 40, were using chairs and pews to bring their opponents to their senses.

"The judge had his clothes torn off his back and, as far as I am concerned, the future of the event lies in the balance."
The Zambia Mail, 11.11.74

The Demon Cold

A talk on *The Evils of Witchcraft*, due to be given by Mrs Doreen Irvine, ex-Queen of the Black Witches, at West Croydon Baptist Church, had to be cancelled.

"It is a great disappointment to us all," said Mr Isaac Whale, a leading Croydon Baptist. "Mrs Irvine is one of the few experts with personal experience of The International Satanist Movement. For many years she stripped for a living under the stage name of Daring Diana. In one quarter, 47 demons were expelled from her."

Mrs Irvine was suffering from a cold.
Croydon Advertiser, 14.12.73

Canon's Salute

A protracted discussion about who should assume a vacant bishopric ended in a gunfight in Teheran between two canons of the Assyrian Catholic Church. As his first Apostolic duty, the survivor said a Requiem over his rival.
Australian Express, 5.4.73

Christening Gift

Holding an about-to-be-baptised infant in one hand, Reverend Spinney of Meltham, West Riding, dipped the other into the font and felt a "foreign body".

Relinquishing the infant, Rev. Spinney found that three pork chops were floating in the holy water.

"It was an unusual event," he said. "Fortunately the ceremony passed off without further hitch. The chops divided nicely between myself and the two church-wardens."
Roswell Daily Record, 7.4.72

Don & Jerry

As part of his Christmas service, the Reverend Don Churchman of St Jude's, Southsea, Hants, held a conversation about the birth of Christ with Jerry, his ventriloquist's dummy, from the pulpit.

"This is not a gimmick," he said.

Jerry, dressed in a choirboy's surplice, was a big hit. Closed circuit television had to be installed in order that the congregational overflow could watch Don's act from an annexe.

Yorkshire Post, 20.12.71

Know Thy Folkestone

After reading the words "ask and it shall be given" in a bible distributed by the Folkestone Biblical Society, Mr Emmanuel Akomeah of Kumasi, Ghana, wrote to the Folkestone Corporation asking them for a copy of the good book.

"We did not have any bibles handy," said a Corporation spokesman, "so we sent him a formal letter of thanks and a copy of the town guide."

Daily Telegraph, 25.2.70

Font of Wisdom

While preaching to his congregation about the dangers of permissive living, the Reverend Anthony Burton of Irby, Lincolnshire, was interrupted by a cry of "Fire!"

Looking smartly about him the vicar discovered that it was he who was alight as, in his passion, he had swayed backwards over a lighted candle.

With considerable presence of mind the vicar left the pulpit and concluded his sermon sitting in a font.

Daily Mail, 20.12.71

Religion on the Run

A failure of the central heating boiler in St Christopher's, Hinchley Wood prompted its vicar, the Reverend Warner, to warm his congregation up by doubling them twice around the church's graveyard while singing the third hymn, Forward For The Lord Of Light.

A spokesman for the Church Association said: "There have been a number of complaints about the sidesman, Mr Pugh, who forgot to ring the bell at the end of the last circuit. Miss Wilmot ran round the church 14 times."
Evening Standard, 26.1.76

Papist Pot

While making their way home after the midnight mass celebrated by the Pope at Drogheda, over 100 people walked into a septic tank.

Mr George Maguire, who installed over 1,000 temporary lavatories for the occasion, said: "I think this proves that God has a sense of humour."
Sunday Independent, 30.9.79

Well Disguised

A keen antiquarian, the Rev. Philip Randall of Eye, Peterborough, fascinated by a stone in his churchyard bearing the initials "HWP" spent eight years searching his parish records for a clue to the sleeper's identity before realising that the letters stood for Hot Water Pipe.
Sunday Mirror, 21.12.69

Quick Answer

Because the Reverend Yeomans of Pontesbury found his congregation singing *I Cannot Help But Wonder Where I'm Bound* in a dull, lifeless manner, he decided to liven things up by dancing in the aisle and "showing them how to put across the message in a bouncy way".

Hardly had they reached the second verse than Reverend Yeomans, waving his arms above his head with devout enthusiasm, vanished through a faulty grille in the church floor into the central heating system.

He got a big laugh.

Daily Mail, 12.5.70

Winning Number

During the main Easter Service in Stockholm Cathedral the officiating minister noticed that the town's Lord Mayor had dozed off during his sermon.

Not wishing to call attention to the Mayor's infirmity, a verger was sent to whisper the number of the closing hymn in his ear.

The congregation was diverted by the sight of their Mayor springing to his feet with a cry of "BINGO!"

Far Eastern Economic Review, 6.3.71

Rock 'n' Roll Over

At a meeting of repentance and renunciation organised by the Aromas Community Baptist Church, Southern California, Messrs David and James Sproule, a pair of leading evangelists from Colorado, persuaded a crowd of several thousand teenagers to smash their rock and roll records to smithereens.

As these enthusiasts pounded their collections to dust, Mr Sproule shouted: "Rock music is the origin of crime, it destroys the central nervous system. No less a man than J. Edgar Hoover has stated that 95 per cent of the four million illegitimate children born in this country were conceived during rock concerts."

After the sermon a weeping Aromas teenager said: "I didn't realise what was going on. To think that I have been attending these concerts for years without knowing the facts."

Rolling Stone, 3.1.72

Pray for Hymn

During the morning service at St Helen's Church, Yorks, the congregation of 60 were surprised when a recently adopted tenor persisted in singing *Praise My Soul The King Of Heaven* three lines ahead of his fellow choristers.

Their surprise turned to amazement as the tenor tore off his surplice and cassock, leapt out of his stall, and began to pelt the faithful with hymn books. "I continued the service as if nothing had occurred," said the Reverend James.

Unappeased by this moderation, the tenor dragged a blind man up onto the altar, mounted the pulpit, and called for silence. At this point the congregation retaliated, pelting the tenor with their own hymnals.

Mr Clark, a worshipper present at the occasion, said: "The man had a wonderful voice."

Guardian, 24.8.70

Fall From Grace

The congregation of the Claymore Memorial Church, Lanarkshire, were not more than halfway through their opening hymn, "Riches Shall Fall From Heaven On High", when a shower of lead strips dropped through the roof, followed by Mr David Raiment, a 35-year-old building inspector, who clutched at the sides of the hole to prevent himself falling among the pews.

Ten strong worshippers held the altar cloth and Mr Raiment allowed himself to drop to safety.

Denying the charge that he had made his way onto the roof in order to steal the lead, Mr Raiment said: "I was taking a short-cut home from an all-night party and I had no idea that I was on top of the church until I heard the organ."

Daily Mail, 2.11.78

Overtaking St Christopher

"I decided to abandon driving and hitch-hike everywhere after my 15th serious car crash," said Mgr Agnello J. Angelini, known in north-eastern Pennsylvania as "The Travellers' Friend".

"Since quitting the wheel I have blessed over 47,000 cars and twice as many drivers," he said. "Driving is the most dangerous activity in the world. Only supernatural intervention can save you."

Police Chief Whalley of Nesquehoning, Pennsylvania, said: "In the spring when the people get their new cars we have up to 3,000 drivers making the journey through mountains of slag, along dangerous, unsurfaced roads to have their windscreens splashed by Mgr Angelini. There are countless accidents and we are trying to get him to move away."

Williamsport Sun-Gazette, 2.11.78

Holy Writ

Because his claim for injuries caused by the collapse of a pavement was dismissed as An Act of God, Mr George Albright decided to sue God for £10,000 damages.

"God", he said, "is widely recognised as the creator of Heaven and Earth and the Churches are his appointed agents."

Mr Albright named 32 churches, synagogues and chapels in his writ.

The Rev. Zilch of Palm Beach said: "I am prepared to give evidence in favour of the principal defendant."
Daily Telegraph, 19.1.68

Catholic Tastes

Mrs Adelaide Douglas, a 91-year-old florist and an assistant to the verger of Mugoorie, Queensland, was shocked when, instead of the luminous statue of the Virgin Mary she had ordered from Ave Enterprises, she received a nine-inch dildo wrapped in a copy of *Sexual Intercourse — The Full Facts*.

Mr Darryl Christmas, the dispatch manager of Ave Enterprises, said: "This is our biggest booboo yet. We deal in sex aids and religious trinkets. We are serious people. We apologise. I am the secretary of the local Vegetarians Against The Nazis group."
The Australian Express, 19.10.79

IN THE COURTS

Crazy Paving

Postmaster Bradbury of Leeds had just finished smoothing the cement of his forecourt when Chip, a local dog, trotted across it.

Mr Bradbury warned Chip off, re-smoothed his cement, and was easing his back when Chip did it again.

Mr Bradbury hurled his shovel at Chip, following it up with a kick. The kick landed on Mrs Rowley, Chip's owner.

Mrs Bradbury, who had observed the incident, decided to call the police. A similar decision was taken by Mrs Rowley.

Mrs Bradbury reached the telephone first. She had dialled the first of three nines when Mrs Rowley pulled her out of the box by her hair.

While settling their differences both ladies fell into the cement.

It was at this point that Mr Bradbury's mother-in-law, Mrs Stevens, decided to intervene. Both she and Mr Bradbury were pulled into the cement by the infuriated wives.

Mrs Stevens is in her late eighties.

Outraged at the behaviour of his neighbours towards his wife, Mr Rowley charged across the road and carried Mr Bradbury and himself back into the cement.

All five citizens then waded into the cement and each other.

The magistrate, Mr Walter Smart, said: "You'd better forget the whole thing."
Anon.

Armed Robbery

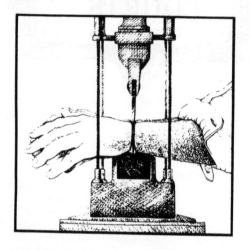

Despairing over his compulsion to steal, Mr Konrad Herrich of Vienna, who had spent 22 of his 44 years in prison for various thefts, put both hands into a machine and severed them from his wrists.

For this he was given four years more.

Sunday Express, 10.5.70

Top Toper

Mr George Linstrum, aged 76, appeared before the Leeds magistrates charged with drunkenness for the 500th time.

"His first appearance was in 1922," said the prosecutor. He was given an absolute discharge.

Two days later he appeared on the same charge for the 501st time. "I was celebrating my anniversary," he said. He was fined 50p.

Guardian, 9.5.71

Mental Fatigue

Explaining his lack of attention at the wheel, Mr Ronald George of Stroud informed the magistrate: "My mind was preoccupied by the thought of my grandson who is in hospital with a broken thigh, my brother who is seriously ill in another hospital, my wife, who is caring for my eighty-eight-year-old mother-in-law and my sister, who has collapsed under the strain of looking after her — to say nothing of the stress involved in the reorganising of local government."

Stroud News and Journal, 4.5.72

Age Concern

Summoned for a breach of the peace, a company director explained to Birmingham magistrates that he often wore unusual clothing: "It relaxes me to wear a black bra under a see-through blouse, panty-hose, silver-plated heels and false eyelashes. Such things are worn every day by the London hippy jet set men. I feel I am being discriminated against on grounds of age."

A police spokesman said: "The defendant is 84."

Daily Mail

51

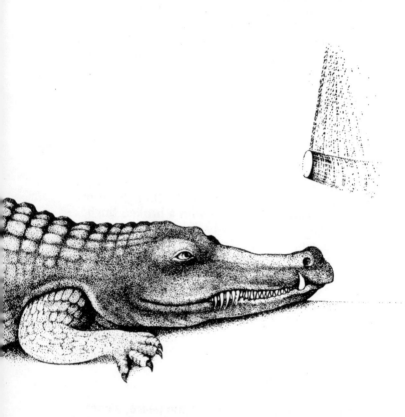

Crocodile Fears

Before going to prison, Mr Shimeon Rimovsky of Tel Aviv asked the magistrate if the court would look after his crocodile.

When the magistrate asked him why he kept the beast, Mr Rimovsky said: "I practise hypnotism on it."

South London Press, 8.1.71

Deaf Aid

Before the Southend magistrates on a charge of assault, Mr Kenneth Thurlow was delighted to hear his neighbour, Mr Arthur Newland — against whom the assault was alleged — say: "In spite of my being punched, I am grateful to Mr Thurlow. He hit me so hard I could hear again."

Mr Newland, aged 61, had been wearing a hearing aid for 20 years.

Essex Chronicle, 11.9.70

Choked!

Armed with a court order forbidding her husband to beat her, Mrs Gloria Judge returned home and flourished the parchment under her husband's nose; whereupon he made her eat it and beat her again.

He was fined £38.

Sunday Times, 6.8.72

The Caught Will Rise

After an eight-week search in which over 6,000 policemen were involved, an escaped convict, Mr Edward Davis, was arrested (dressed as a woman) in the public gallery of Bradford Magistrates' Court while listening to the trial of his grandmother, Mrs Ada Gristle, for drunken driving.

To complete his disguise, Mr Davis was holding a two-year-old girl on his lap.

Guardian, 22.11.73

Scout's Honour

Arrested for urinating on the public highway, Mr
William Ferry of Plaistow explained that he was not guilty
because, before urinating, he had tacked a notice reading
'GENTLEMEN' to a nearby tree.
"I always carry it with me in case of need," he said.
The Prestwich & Whitfield Guide, 19.3.76

Teacher's Petty Thief

Asked how she could make so positive an identification
of Fergus Wayne, charged by the Cleveland, Ohio, police
with robbing her home, Miss Dolores Niggle, a retired
school-mistress of 81, said:

"After he had been through my handbag, Mr Wayne
came over to the bed. It was then that we recognized each
other. He was one of my favourite pupils in 1925.

"He bent over and gave me a kiss, saying: 'You were
always kind to me'."
Evening News, 12.4.75

Greek Mythology

Charged with a $42 million social security fraud, 153 Australian Greeks, plus their wives, their children and their lawyers assembled in a Sydney court only to be informed that the team of prosecutors had asked for a further year's adjournment because the police had been unable to sort out which of the accused was which.

Prior to the adjournment being granted, Mr Clive Evatt QC rose to his feet and admitted that he could not pronounce his client's name. Several women shouted the client's name out, one of them adding, "He committed suicide six months ago!"

During the pandemonium that followed this announcement, Mr Walter George and Miss Erika Clooney, both solicitors, found they had been briefed to defend the same man and, harangued by a group of the accused, began to fight each other for the papers.

Leaping into the well of the court, another man, who identified himself as "Achilles X", floored Mr George and held Miss Clooney's hand aloft, shouting, "This is the one for me!"

When things had calmed down, Miss Clooney said she had never seen the man before although she "had known him well for over a year".

"I would have done my best to get the trial under way," said Judge Griffin. "However, among the accused we found a Mrs Chong Wah Wong-Diamantopoulos who admitted that her husband was among the crowd but was unable to identify him at short notice."

The Age, 13.6.78

Gael Farce

Interesting linguistic problems arose during the case brought by Miss Honor Tracy of Achill Island, Co. Mayo, against Mr Michael O'Donnell, a gentleman of the same island.

Suing Mr O'Donnell for allowing his horses to trample on her *Gunnera Mantica*, Miss Tracy said that she had written twice to him about the nuisance but her letters had made not the slightest difference.

Mr O'Donnell, who defended himself in Gaelic, said that he could not read foreign languages.

When he tried to question Miss Tracy, she said: "Stop talking gibberish. I have seen plenty of stage Irishmen, but I never heard of, or from, one so stupid as to make up a language to go with it."

Mr O'Donnell *(in Gaelic)*: "Ireland forever!"

Miss Tracy *(in English)*: "What about my *Gunnera Mantica*?"

Mr O'Donnell *(in Gaelic)*: "Another foreigner."

Miss Tracy *(in English)*: "Most of your horses come from Wales."

District Judge McGahon said: "The Constitution allows both languages to be spoken in court. However, as the summons was for a day in December and the evidence concerns a day in January I have no option but to dismiss the charge."

After the case Miss Tracy said: "Now I've heard everything." *(In English.)*

Irish Times, 19.9.73

Collector's Punch

For four years Mr Sidney Baker, a ticket collector at Folkestone Central, said "Good night, Bill," to a particular passenger as he surrendered his ticket and left the platform.

One evening, while Mr Baker was uttering these words, the man punched him in the throat, putting him off work for three weeks.

"My name is not Bill, it's Arthur," Mr. A. Drake explained to the magistrate.
Daily Mail, May 1969

Mayoral Rogue

A man who made a two-finger gesture at a High Court judge later apologised in the Teesside Crown Court.

He said he had mistaken the judge for the Mayor of Teesside.

The apology was accepted and the man released.
Daily Telegraph, 20.7.73

No Jury Vetting

A trial for attempted murder being held in Manitoba was discontinued after Mr John Bunn, one of the jury, rose to his feet and asked Mr Justice J.R. Solomon, presiding, to speak up.

An enquiry revealed that Mr Bunn was very deaf and that his fellow juryman, Mr Henry Thorn, was totally deaf.

Further enquiries revealed that three other members of the jury could not understand English.

Mr Thorn admitted that he thought he was hearing a divorce case, while Mr Jaiy Igawar had come to the courthouse in order to apply for a pistol permit.
Toronto Globe & Mail, 11.2.76

Slack Bencher

During the longest-running trial in the Court's history, Mr Wayne Southam, for the defence, made a dramatic appeal for the case to be abandoned because the judge had been asleep for over two hours.

"Nor is this the only occasion on which I have been prompted to the foregoing allegation," he continued. "The court official in question has been slumped over his arms with both his eyes closed on no less than 16 occasions in the last 63 days.

"I agree that the cross-examinations, particularly my own, have been exceptionally boring. Last Thursday, which you will remember was particularly hot, the judge appeared to fall asleep on four occasions — before and after lunch. Acting on his example, I noticed eight of the jurymen in a similar posture.

"I know that the judge and jury slept during the trial of Robert Emmet; that, however, was during the summing-up. But how can a judge who is asleep assess the credibility of a witness?

"The judge may reply that he was only simulating sleep the better to evaluate the evidence. But justice must be seen to be done."

Supporting his colleague's allegation, Mr McTeenie said that on one occasion he had asked for a "toilet adjournment" in order for the judge to be apparently woken up from his apparent sleep.

Evening Press, 26.4.78

Rhyming Slanging Match

Only two months after he was bound over to keep the peace, the Islington poet George McPhee was arrested for screaming.

"I had had a bad day," he told the magistrate, Mr St. John Hawser. "Browsing in Harrod's book department, I earmarked a copy of Fulke Greville's *Collected Works*, went to have a quick look at the Children's Bookshelf, and when I got back an Arab had snapped up the Greville.

"Then I went for a drink with a social worker who consumed 28 glasses of beer and, having invited her home, I found I could not get rid of her. So I began to scream."

"McPhee was screaming when we arrived at the flat," said Sergeant Frank Turner. "When we questioned the social worker about her reasons for refusing to leave the flat, she explained that she was McPhee's wife."
Hampstead & Highgate Express, 25.7.78

Hypocrisy Exposed

Supported by crutches, Mr Graham Firth of Shipley, Yorks told the magistrate that he became involved with four waiters from Pinkies, a London restaurant, after he had been asked to leave because he was not wearing a tie.

"Under normal circumstances I would have left without saying a word," he said, "but as it was a topless restaurant I thought they were going a bit far."
Camden & St Pancras Chronicle, 7.6.74

False Evidence

On being asked if there was any truth in the charge of drunkenness brought against him, Mr Bailie removed his dentures and threw them at the magistrate, crying: "I have never been drunk in my life!"

He was fined £1.
Hackney Gazette, 20.1.70

Reigning Shit

Cal Cavendist, the country-and-western singer, was charged by the Royal Canadian Mounted Police with dropping a manure-bomb on the local golf club's pavilion.

"He buzzed the pavilion a couple of times," said Captain Henry, "and on his third run he threw two carrier-bags filled with horse-shit over the members and their friends."
The Edmonton Journal, 24.4.75

Birth Right

While on trial for theft, Mrs Farida Halim gave birth to a seven-pound boy in the dock. Without hesitation, she named him Bara — "not guilty" in Arabic. The case was adjourned.
The Sun, 30.1.71

Disarmed Robbery

Entering a strong plea of mitigation on behalf of his plaintiff, Mr Joshua Obo said: "The man is basically innocent. Upon entering the bank he subsequently robbed, he got his foot jammed in the revolving door and had to be helped to the counter by the lady he then threatened. On being told that the till did not contain the £5,000 for which he asked, he reduced his demands, first to £500, then to £50, and finally to £5 and the offer of a drink around the corner."

The Scotsman, November 1975

Judge and Juryman

"Now I am known as Jocular John," said Mr George Wade of Bisley.

This nickname derives from a brush between Mr Wade and Judge Smythers. Mr Wade, a juryman, was heard to say, "Cheer up, mush, we'll get you off," as he passed the dock in which Mr Harry Spice, a dealer, stood downcast.

"I was only giving the time of day," said Mr Wade, "when the Judge looked up and said 'Take him below'.

"Taken below, a barrister was sent down to me. I heard him say, 'Where is the chap that's going to get ten years?' before he came into my cell.

"Three hours later the Judge had me up and I explained to him that I am a simpleton who likes to have a friendly word with a stranger now and again.

"I don't reckon they keep a straight face through the ages, I told him. Then, to my surprise, they stuffed 16 quid into my hand and sent me home in a police car.

"I suppose they were frightened that I might speak to the world's press."

Western Mail, 10.6.76

Top Secrets

Madame Ivy Canon, char-woman to the Minister of War, was sentenced to two years in prison and a fine of £500 for covering her jam-pots with top secret military documents.
Anon, 1965

Pregnancy Skare

The Supreme Court of Sweden ruled that Dagmar Bjorn, a 75-year-old postman, was the father of Johannes Tyce, a 54-year-old dog breeder, by Katheryn Sluurd, a 92-year-old agricultural labourer.

Ms Sluurd told the court: "I was hoeing a turnip field in Southern Skare in 1924 when a cyclist arrived, dismounted his machine and became the father of my child."

Asked how she could recognise Mr Bjorn after so long an interval, Ms Sluurd replied, "Because of his exceptional ugliness."
Daily Telegraph, 23.3.78

Liquor Licence

Mr Keith Hooper, a voter from Honiton, Devon, was fined £20 for displaying a Guinness Stout label instead of a road fund licence.
Daily Telegraph

Stumped!

The headmaster of St John's, Churt, was accused of beating a pupil with his artificial leg for dancing the wrong way around a maypole.
Daily American, 23.1.76

Mercy Killing

In court for poaching, Mr David Turple of Musselburgh explained:

"Sheriff, I shot that pheasant because it was looking ill."

Scotsman, 4.2.70

Shagged Out

After being bound over to keep the peace for two years, Mr George Chilie, a car salesman of Wiltshire, told an interviewer that winding down the window of his Rolls-Royce and shouting "Shagger!" at Mrs Daphne Morris and her two children was "merely a kind greeting for old time's sake" and had "absolutely nothing to do with sex in any shape or form".

"We are very old friends," said Mr Chilie. "We were at school together. I know her mind like the back of my hand. Had I realised that my shouting 'Shagger!' as I happened to drive past would give any offence, I would have chosen a different word to express my thoughts."

Mrs Morris said: "This is the sixth occasion on which the defendant has yelled 'Shagger!' at me and my two children — neither of which belong to him. Sometimes he pounds his horn and bounces up and down at the wheel of his big ugly car. I don't mind him shouting 'Shagger!' at me because I am innocent. But my young ones react badly. During the last incident of this kind, Ivory (aged 3) shouted 'Shagger yourself!' and Carole (aged 2) joined in with 'Dad!' "

Surrey Advertiser, 18.5.73

Grave Consequences

Mr Grumpin told the court that his wife Elizabeth had been praying beside the grave that contained all that was left of her two sisters when its stone toppled over and trapped her.

"It took five hours to get her free," he said. "I found the incident upsetting because my wife's nephew was crushed to death by a similar gravestone two years ago."
Daily Mail, October 1977

Adult Education

"I have been watching *Jackanory* through Thompsons' window for the last three months and I did not want to miss a single moment of it," said Mrs Brenda Winkle of Eastbourne. "Thompsons' placed the set in the window for customer-benefit," she continued, "and I have been shopping there for over 30 years."

Mrs Winkle was charged with using a pair of scissors as an offensive weapon after stabbing Miss Joan Naylor in the bottom.

"She and her friend were at the front of the crowd watching *Jackanory*. They kept bobbing about and I could not see a thing. In any case, she's 20 and I'm 73 so I am allowed to teach her a lesson."
Evening Argus 10.11.77

Robber Barren

Awarding Mr Philip Mc-Cutcheon a conditional discharge and a total of 90 hours community service work, Mr Rodney Percy, the Recorder at York Crown Court, said: "I think you should give burglary up. You have a withered hand, an artificial leg and only one eye. You have been caught in Otley, Leeds, Harrogate, Norwich, Beverley, Hull and York. How can you hope to succeed?"
Guardian, 21.1.77

Arturo Who?

"I did it! I did it!" cried Miss Ida Rubell during her trial for abducting, killing, plucking, cooking and serving with rice to her 96-year-old mother a Panamanian parrot called Arturo.

"Arturo was no ordinary bird," said his owner, Mr Robert P. Zing. "He spoke three languages, ate scrambled eggs and he had a small but varied repertoire of 19th century love songs."

Mr Zing admitted that eight years ago a dog Miss Rubell claimed as her own had died while in his company. "But it was a very old dog and not at all well-educated."

Milwaukee Journal, 2.9.79

COURTSHIP

Nassa Project

Mr David Jeremy, a carpenter of Merthyr Tydfil, was fined £18 for attempting to obtain a passport in the name of Nassa Ocovish.

"I fell in love with Miss Jane Plum at first sight," he said. "When she told me that she was interested in foreigners I told her that I was the son of a Puerto Rican uranium miner called Nassa Ocovish — a name that just came into my mind. For two years she has known me as Nassa. Whenever we went out I had to pick places where I was unknown. But there were always people around who used to shout 'Hullo Dave' and things like that. Finally I decided to get a document that would prove who I was, but it was my undoing."
Daily Telegraph, 8.8.79

Uncivil Action

The Sheriff of Doncaster was fined £20 for brawling with a couple aged 77 and 83 who were "canoodling" under the window of the bedroom in which he (the Sheriff) was trying to sleep "after a long and tiring day of civic duties".
Sheffield Star, 4.11.75

Low Calibre Love

"I have decided to call it all off," said Mr M.J. Hubbard of Akron, Ohio after his bride-to-be, Miss Sadie Moss, admitted to shooting him in the leg.

"We have been living together for 14 years and during that time she has shot me 33 times," he continued.

The Akron police confirmed that this was the case, although up until now Mr Hubbard has never preferred charges.

"This time I'm turning her in," he said.

Miss Moss explained that she was a crack shot and "only inflicted minor ·22 flesh wounds — and then only if we have a real flare-up."

Denver Post, 14.2.76

Tyrone's Power

Two days after he collapsed while finishing the Saudi Arabian leg of his Round-The-World-Love-March, Mr Wayne Eyemouth of Peekie, Oregon, was transferred to an intensive care unit when he heard that Ms Shelley Ziz, with whom he fell in love at first sight in 1974, had married his younger brother, Tyrone.

"Our eyes crossed while we were studying a methane contract issued by the Oregon Natural Gas Company," he said. "From that moment on I have been able to think of nothing but Shelley."

During her interview, Ms Ziz revealed that Mr Eyemouth had declared his love for her by erecting a thirty-foot-high cardboard heart on the roof of his bungalow. When she declined his proposal, he set out to walk around the world, asking those he met to sign a petition begging her to change her mind.

"I decided to marry Tyrone after the first 10,000 signatures arrived in Peekie," she said.

The Daily Gleaner, 20.3.78

Tender Trap

As a part-time fireman who was having difficulties with his girl friend, Mr Peter Monckton telephoned the station at which he worked and told them of a fictitious fire at the school where she worked.

"I wanted to see her very badly," he said.

Unfortunately, though the Brigade sent two engines and nine men, they did not include Mr Monckton.

"I wanted to ride on the water tender," he said.

Birmingham Evening Mail, 21.1.70

Fate Worse Than Death

Despairing of his chances to win the affection of Miss Sheila Mindon, Mr Barry Hitchen, a railway worker, decided to take his own life.

"At 7.30 I had a drink and walked into the sea," he said, "but it was so wet I turned back, went home and by 9.15 I had wired up my easy chair to the mains. However, each time I threw the switch the power fused. Following this, I broke my Gayeaway mirror and tried to cut my wrists, yet somehow the slashes were not deep enough. After that I tried to hang myself from the bannisters; unfortunately the knot was improperly tied. Finally I surrounded myself with cushions and set them on fire. This method was much too hot, so I jumped out of the window and telephoned the Samaritans but they were constantly engaged."

Miss Mindon said: "I quite like Barry, but his idea of courtship is a bit odd. When I arrived at the station and asked him how long the next train would be, he said, 'Two coaches'. When I came back from having a cup of tea he had blown his whistle and the train had gone."

Whitley Bay Guardian, 3.11.78

CRIME

Sanguine Clot

Confirming that Mr Michael Maryn of Passaic, New Jersey had been mugged 83 times during the past five years, Detective Andrew Risko said: "He is not a trouble-maker. He just happens to be in the wrong place at the wrong time."

Mr Maryn was shot (twice), stabbed, coshed with a pipe, lost a part of one ear, had his nose broken, his rib-cage smashed and his skull fractured.

In addition to these injuries, he lost over $2,000, several bags of groceries and four cars.

"I don't worry about it," he said. "You only live once. I'm lucky in one respect — I have a blood clot in my leg that keeps me from travelling far from home."

Detroit Free Press, 25.7.77

Bristol Rovers

While giving a lecture entitled "Law and Order — Is This the End?", Mr James Pennant said that he had found the people of Bristol to be incurably dishonest.

"On leaving my car for a matter of a few seconds in order to relieve myself in a dark corner, a tape-recording of my grandmother's funeral was stolen from the play slot. And while I was answering nature's call my pocket was picked."

Bristol Evening Post, 20.4.78

Artificial Aim

While they were waiting at a bus stop in Clerimston, Mr and Mrs Daniel Thirsty were threatened by a Mr Robert Clear.

"He demanded that I give him my wife's purse," said Mr Thirsty. "Telling him that the purse was in her basket, I bent down, put my hands up her skirt, detached her artificial leg and hit him over the head with it. It was not my intention to do any more than frighten him off but, unhappily for us all, he died."

Edinburgh Evening News, 18.8.78

Against the Odds

Mr Dam Saeng Dung of Prakomchai District, Brui Dam, near Bangkok, joined a group of friends for a game of cards in a deserted hut outside the village of Jimgo.

One of his fellow gamblers, Mr Vichien Benjawan, was the alleged thief of Mr Dung's watch.

Halfway through the game, the police burst through the curtains and shot Mr Dung.

"We have apologised to Mr Dung's family," said a police spokesperson. "When Mr Dung informed us of his rendezvous with the notorious thief Benjawan, he unfortunately enclosed a photograph of himself rather than the criminal."
Bangkok Post, 1.5.76

Low Trick

After several weeks of searching, the bank squad of Phoenix, Arizona arrested a professional wrestler, Mr Raymond McCray, in connection with a £45,000 robbery.

Mr McCray, a three and a half foot dwarf, was able to avoid surveillance cameras because his head remained below the counter.
Daily Express, 31.5.73

Hood Manners

Mr Clarence Ramsay was standing on the pavement outside his home in Houston, Texas, when a man came up and stabbed him in the back. Turning round to face his assailant, Mr Ramsay was surprised to hear him say, "Sorry — I thought you were somebody else."
Western Evening Herald

Cover Blown

Having filched a sheepskin coat from the lobby of the hotel he was passing, Mr Sam Thomas of Yarmouth, England thumbed a lift from a passing coach. To his surprise it was filled with 40 Detective Chief Inspectors of Police returning from a crime seminar at Bognor.

After two minutes, one of the Inspectors felt the collar of Mr Thomas's coat and declared it to be his own.

"I realised that I had made a terrible mistake," Mr Thomas said.

He was driven to the nearest police station.
7.3.75

EMPLOYMENT

Sock Therapy

Mr James Madams of Wellington, New Zealand was hurled 20 feet into the air while holding his wheelbarrow. The explosion, caused by an underground gas leak, gave him no great discomfort.

"I just took a few minutes off to let my socks settle down," he said.

Last July Mr Madams drove a steel spike into an 11,000 volt cable. "I wasn't hurt at all," he said.

New Zealand Herald, 18.11.69

What a Pickle!

The suit by Mrs Jo Heeber, a secretary, demanding $1 million from her employer for his insistence that she danced naked as part of her professional skills, but did not demand the same service from his male employees, was dropped after Mr Robert Hose, the accused, died in the witness box while eating a pickled onion.
Evening Argus, 12.1.78

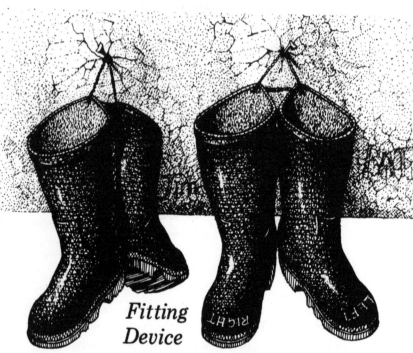

Fitting Device

A strike was called at a McAlpine building site.
Whereas the gumboots issued to the local labourers were unmarked, those given to the Irish were marked 'left' and 'right'.
Contract Journal, May 1975

Foot and Mouth

Giving evidence to an industrial tribunal against her former assistant Miss Brenda Walker, Mrs Louise Boverton, manageress of the Ladies Footwear Market, Chester, said: "Brenda's sales technique was unusual. If our extensive stock failed to satisfy a potential customer, Brenda would say that it was the customer's own fault for having splay feet, or a hammer toe, or bubble insteps. On one occasion she told a prospective buyer to 'Piss off home and wash 'em'. Hearing this pit-language I discharged her on the spot."

At this point, Mr John Carder, a member of the tribunal, interrupted Mrs Boverton's evidence to say that he had been a miner for over 30 years and that never in his life had he heard such language used below surface level.

Miss Walker was given £170 compensation.
Daily Express, 10.1.79

Hard Times

A cook from Peterborough lost his claim for redundancy pay when he admitted it took him 30 minutes to boil an egg.
Daily Mail, 30.5.70

Corny Problem

When Mr Lorenzo Guarnieri of Palermo read of a Spanish waiter who had twenty-four toes, he said, "So what? I have twenty-six."

"In fact," he went on, "my family have 78 between us — and that's only three people, including myself."

Mr Guarnieri, who was unemployed, suggested that a film producer might be interested in starring him in a picture where the police are baffled by a villain who leaves twenty-six toe-prints.
Anon.

Allelooya Chorus

Upwards of fifty well-wishers crowded into the ladies' lavatory at St Paul's Cray, Kent to bid farewell to Mrs Alice Gilbert who was retiring after 45 years as chief attendant.

Alice, known to her regulars as Mrs Loo, handed round drinks, cakes and sandwiches. The ceremony ended with everyone joining in a chorus of:

"Goodbye, Mrs Loo,
We're sorry to be leaving you,
Boo-hoo!"

During the closing bars all the toilets were flushed in unison.

Daily Mirror, 9.2.73

ENTERTAINMENT

Sweet Squirt of Success

Diners at the Golden Egg restaurant, Colchester, had their meals enlivened when a young man picked up a large plastic tomato and squirted its sauce content all over a lady who was seated next to him.

This done, he threw the tomato across the room, crossed the street and entered a Wimpy Bar where other condemned souls were undergoing nourishment.

After looking about, he climbed onto the bar and picked up a plastic coconut whose contents he squirted over the cakes and the barman, cried "Good Evening!" (although it was only afternoon), and withdrew to a nearby pub.

Asked why he had done these things, he answered:

"I wanted to read something amusing in the local paper."

Essex County Standard, 10.5.68

Party Pooper

Raiding a party in Santiago on its third day, the local police discovered a dead man, "sitting quietly in a corner"

Asked to explain, Mr Miguel Cookson, the host, said: "He was a gate-crasher called Jose. We discovered that he was dead on Saturday evening; not wanting to spoil the party, we decided to leave him where he was until Monday morning."

Oldham Evening Chronicle, 3.5.78

Silent Night

A Los Angeles record company issued an LP entitled 'The Best of Marcel Marceau'. Each side had 20 minutes of stereophonic silence followed by 20 seconds of applause.

Mr Viner, the company's director, said: "The record has been so successful we are planning a second volume for Christmas. We will use the same pressing but have a completely different sleeve."
Daily Telegraph, 5.8.70

Strains of Music

"My husband takes an interest in popular music," said Mrs Wendy Lowe of Ipswich. "When I saw that Brian Meadway's latest disc included a personal offer from him to perform in the home of his admirers, I wrote away giving him the date of our wedding anniversary and our address.

"The doorbell went just after supper, and my husband, to whom I had not mentioned the matter, went to the door.

"Much to his surprise, Mr Meadway, who was quite drunk, pushed his way in, said he had been detained at a press conference, and spent 20 minutes in the lavatory. After this, he joined my husband and his mother (who had come from Torquay for the occasion) and insisted on borrowing my tennis racquet to mime the song properly. When he began, the neighbours knocked on the wall to stop the noise. Whereupon Mr Meadway pounded back with the racquet and shouted obscenities up the chimney.

"On the way out he was sick all over the hall carpet, and when I told him he had spoiled our evening, he said: 'That's showbusiness'."

Anon

Yesterday's Witness

"It was a very warm day," said Mrs Harriet Cole, "so we decided to celebrate my grandmother-in-law's birthday in the yard. My sons carried the cake with its 97 candles outside and we all stood around the table while I lit them. As Mrs Yesterday — our pet name for Harry's gran — was not up to blowing the candles out, Harry decided to do the honours. He drew a huge breath and expelled it suddenly over the candles. But he went at it so seriously it blew gran off her feet and into the dustbin. It took us 15 minutes to get her out."
South Wales Echo, 12.8.52

What Bullshit!

"Because we have some of the world's most beautiful women living hereabouts," said Mayor Cronkie, "we decided to put the Miss Kawartha Lakes Natural Loveliness Competition into orbit by holding the first-ever Canadian bull-fight season to precede the judging. It was a disaster.

"We imported six Mexican bulls and two Mexican bull-fighters. Our laws prohibit cruelty to animals so it was decided that if a bullfighter touched a bull between the horns the contest would be over. The bulls arrived on time but were found to be infested with ticks, so they had to be quarantined for a week, which meant the show was delayed.

"A bakery that had prepared three thousand tortillas went broke; four impromptu calypso bands declared themselves to be homeless people; and a local woman went on the radio to say that she would commit suicide if the bulls were not released.

"When the day arrived it was discovered that one of the bullfighters had married and his wife refused to allow him to perform in the ring. The other bullfighter turned out to be a drunkard. Only 14 people turned up, six of whom were from the Ontario Society for the Prevention of Cruelty to Animals.

"It was then that Police Chief Hogan decided that he would face the first bull. The chief — a 600lb, 6ft 4in human — entered the ring and walked up to the bull, who knocked him down. Nothing daunted, Chief Hogan got to his feet, brushed the dirt of his jacket, and the bull knocked him down again.

"Dazed though he was, the Chief drew himself erect and, I regret to say, the bull's third charge hospitalized him.

"As his daughter, May Hogan, was last year's Miss Kawartha Lakes, she rode in the ambulance with him, taking the crown along, so the Natural Loveliness Competition was cancelled.

"Our final problem came with the bull, which nobody knew how to corral. However, after a short conference between themselves, the OSPCA team decided that something had to be done and so their President shot it dead — with an approved weapon.

"I have resigned my office and when anybody asks me where I come from I say Omenee, which is where my mother was born in 1939."
The Daily Gleaner, 30.8.78

Taking a Stand

Mr V.S. Anandan, a Sri Lankan Professor of Ancient Greek, increased the world record for standing on one leg from 8 hours 46 minutes to 12 hours 47 minutes.

During his ordeal, which was watched by a crowd of several thousand unemployed people, the Professor, who weighs 135 pounds, passed the time by reciting passages from the works of Aristophanes.
Daily Mail, August 1978

The Mouse Trap

"I had no desire to see *Carrie* myself, but my wife insisted upon it," said Mr Jim Wedding of Clacton.

After being led from the Apollo cinema in a state of shock, Mr Wedding explained that it was not because of anything in the film that he had torn off his trouser leg and stuffed it into the cinema manager's mouth.

"It was a dull film — just as I expected it to be. But during one of the so-called 'nerve-tingling' sequences a mouse ran up the leg of my trousers," he said.
East London Advertiser

In Her Own Write

The Horndale Public Library Committee issued a circular in which they asked ticket-holders not to use rashers of bacon and kipper spines as bookmarks.

A library spokesman said: "We have had a number of complaints from borrowers about such incidents. The most unusual came from a lady who found 'GONE FOR CHIPS — BACK IN FIVE MINUTES' written in lipstick across the title page of Arthur Askey's memoirs."
Evening Standard, 7.7.75

The Naked Lie

While she was minding her own business, Mrs Theresa Eddon, a Farworth (near Pickering) mother of six, heard screams coming from a nearby tree under which there stood two distressed women.

The women were pointing at a naked man coming from the woods.

Mrs Eddon invited the women inside and confronted the naked man.

He said: "I am a descendant of Isaiah and this valley is due for development."

Mrs Eddon told him that she had heard nothing about it.

The man said he wanted some clothes.

Mrs Eddon brought him some clothes, which he said did not suit him.

Then he re-entered the woods in the direction of Pickering.

Malvern Gazette, 29.3.74

A Chile Wind. . .

During a performance of Rigoletto in Chile, Louis Quilico, a Canadian baritone, fainted after swallowing a pigeon's feather that wafted down from the roof.

When the front-of-house manager went onstage to apologise for Mr Quilico's indisposition he tripped over the soprano's dress and dove into the orchestra.

Ottawa Globe & Mail, 22.8.70

Royal Command

Engaged by Mohammed Fal, Master of Ceremonies of the Court of Jeddah, to perform at the birthday party of Prince Aziz, Mr George Turner (known professionally as "Merlin the Magnificent") said:

"Knowing that royalty would be present I was determined to give everything I could. Then Mr Fal told me that I could not use my Guillotine Yourself At Home illusion — the best in my act.

"I replied that perhaps it would be better if, as the high point of the show, we stoned a rabbit to death; whereupon I was instantly deported."

Sunday Mirror, 29.1.78

Grin and Bare It

Three Stockholm couples who attended the first night of *Oh! Calcutta!* in the nude were surprised when the house manager threw them out.

"We understood that you had to be in the nude in order to get in," they said.

Evening News, 23.8.71

Rearguard Action

Just before he began to compete in a horse-shoeing contest before the Queen, Mr Norman Rose, a blacksmith from Toronto, was told that at no time must the horse's rear be allowed to face Her Majesty.

"The effect of this order", Mr Rose said, "was disastrous for me. The Queen was taking a keen interest in the competition and kept on walking around the horse I was shoeing. Every time she went near its rear I had to hop, hop, hop it around away from her."
The Sun, 28.6.73

Nota Bene

In compliance with the composer's instructions the house lights of Bergen's concert hall were switched off during a performance of *Concerto In C* by Terry Riley, given by Miss Siri None and The Harmonia Symphony Orchestra. The *Concerto* has an uncomplicated score: a single note is repeated for 20 minutes.

When the lights came up Miss None discovered that the conductor, Mr Lucas Foss, the orchestra, and the audience, had left.
Daily Sketch, 3.12.70

GARDENING

Tiny Mind

Mr James Scott, a fashionable
dentist and bonsai fancier, has
succeeded in growing a minia-
ture oak tree in a hollow tooth.
The Sun, 10.10.70

Oak-lined Coffers

Arboretum proprietors noted with interest the gardening habits of Sheikh Zaid of Abu Dhabi. Having constructed a nine-lane, ten-mile long drive to his new Gulf-side palace, the Sheikh chose to line it with twenty-five-year-old oaks.

Within ten weeks of planting, the trees died. They were, however, replaced five times a year.

Twenty-five thousand twenty-five-year-old oaks cost the Sheikh £1,600,000.

A bargain.

Sunday People, 24.6.73

Liquid Manure

Mr Derek Cook of Pirton, Hertfordshire was awarded a prize for his 85-pound pumpkin in spite of its having split sides.

"I feed it on ferret-dung and Guinness," he said.

Sun, 15.10.71

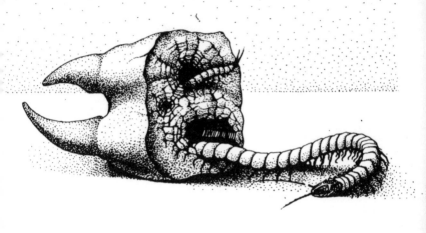

Flora and Fauna

When Mr Barnet Kopkin, a dentist of Stoke
Newington, had pulled one of Mrs Ruth Abraham's
teeth, a centipede uncurled itself from within a
tooth and walked around his operating tray.

"It may have been there for quite some time,"
said Mr Kopkin. "Such events are quite unusual, of
course, but I once had a patient in whose mouth a
tomato seed had begun to grow into a small plant."
Times, 5.10.72

GAY NEWS

My Man Bobette

From a letter to the *Calgary Herald*:

"As a woman who is married to a transvestite, I want to thank you for pointing out that men who enjoy dressing up in women's clothes are not necessarily homosexual.

"My Bob is all man. He stands six foot two inches tall and weighs 190 pounds. After the children are asleep he puts on high heels, false eyelashes and a wig before slipping into a negligee. I call him my Bobette and we both look forward to these wonderful moments in our life. He is a different person. He even finds the jokes on television much funnier."
Calgary Herald, 31.12.68

Instructor Backfires

Mr G. Ambrose, a pupil of the British School of Motoring and of Cambridge University, was stunned when his instructor emitted what Mr Ambrose later described as "a cataclysmic fart".

Lighting Mr Ambrose's cigarette, the instructor then said: "I think you should know that I am queer and that it is nothing to be ashamed of. It says on the card that you are called Ambrose. Can I call you Ambrosia?"

Soon after this the instructor lurched forward onto the dashboard, saying, "Christ, am I pissed!"

A spokesperson for the motoring school said that the instructor had been placed on indefinite sick leave.

Anon.

HOUSING

Sewage Disposal

"We had been getting on quite well with the Browns," said Mrs Eunice Chick, "until this unfortunate occurrence.

"After our lavatory became completely blocked I called the Council. They were round in next to no time in their lorry. They went into number 40 (our house) and inserted their biggest pump into our convenience. One of the council operatives switched it on. There was a tremendous rumble. Janet, my five-year-old, thought it was thunder. This rumble was followed by a tremendous whoosh. I nipped upstairs and flushed the convenience. It was working perfectly.

"No sooner had the operatives vanished than I saw June Brown from number 42 coming up the garden path. She was hysterical. Apparently, when the pump began to work, instead of sucking it blew, and the whole of Mrs Brown's bedroom suite was covered with effluvia."

The Council are to blame," said Mr Bob Brown. "We are camping out at June's parents. Our house is ruined. It's everywhere. The ceilings are in danger of collapsing. The lavatory pan was blown into the spare bedroom and the TV is all clogged up."

Eastbourne Council held a full investigation.
Daily Mail, 12.5.75

Dun Roamin'

Found asleep in the bedding department of All Things Worldwide Hypermarket, Chicago, Mrs Mandy Palm, a widow of 73, explained that she had been in the giant store for over a month because she could not find her way to the exit.

"After the first day I asked a detective the way out," she said. "But he told me that I looked like a tramp and if I didn't get out he would arrest me on suspicion.

"After that I opened an account and lived off the things I bought, eating in the restaurants and taking a bath at night. I had no one to telephone and soon got used to the new routine."

Glasgow Herald, 18.4.79

Vanity Unit Collapses

Miss Eleanor Barry, a 70-year-old actress, was smothered to death by a collection of personal newspaper clippings that fell on her while she was alone in her New York flat.
The Times, December 1977

Insecure Tenor

Mrs Joanna Volger of Buchrain, a village near Lucerne, has been obliged to move house eight times in thirteen years.

In spite of being a clean and reliable tenant, her landlords was forced to evict her because of neighbourly complaints about her voice.

Addressing her husband or her children in a normal way, the sound she produced registered 80 decibels. Exactly the same number of decibels was registered when the meter was placed beside a working circular saw.

Eugene, her 11-year-old son, said: "Usually Mother speaks in a low whisper, but every so often she forgets herself and switches to her normal volume; soon after that we are out."
Daily Telegraph, 14.2.70

Neighbores

Forty-three residents of Linenhall Square, Newry, Armagh signed a petition asking for a local family to be removed because "they are a moral danger to children living in the area".

They were keeping a horse in one of the bedrooms.

"We won it in a raffle," said the wife. "There was not a proper stable so it had to go in with the kids. Nobody complained until these council busybodies stuck their noses in".

Armagh Observer, 16.9.67

Squeals on Wheels

Mr John Whitedriver of Santa Ana, California was arrested for sharing his caravan with a donkey, three grizzly bears, 13 dogs, three rabbits, an ocelot, a bobcat, nine chickens, two opossums, three peacocks, 16 quail, five pigs, five doves, six pigeons, a monkey, a woman and eight children. He was charged with cruelty to animals.

Daily Mail

IN MEMORIAM

Mournful Motoring

"So many people want to come by and view the remains — but they just don't have the time. This way they can drive by and just keep on going," said Mr Hirschel Thornton of Atlanta, discussing his new Drive-In Mortuary.

Five 6-foot windows were opened in the wall of Mr Thornton's funeral home, which faced onto a busy street. "They'll be lying there conveniently tilted towards the callers," he went on. "A skilful driver won't need to stop — just change right down and coast by.

"A surprising number of mourners like to view late at night — our fluorescent systems are on 24 hours a day. Midnight to 1.00 a.m. seems to be favourite. I dunno — maybe they work late."

Another advantage of Mr Thornton's system was that people didn't have to dress up to see the remains. "They can come in their pyjamas if they want to," he said.

Asked if he feared traffic jams in so busy an area, Mr Thornton admitted that it was probable, "but experience has shown that vulgar curiosity seekers soon tire".

Each window was fitted with wall-to-wall carpeting, drapes, floral remembrances, and a neon sign giving the occupant's name and date of burial.
Baltimore Sun

Better than Frying. . .

"My husband was a man who believed in work," said Mrs Joan Moyse of West Ealing. "Just before he died he said how much he would like to continue paying his way when he had gone. My daughter and I thought about this and after his cremation we took his ashes home with us, ground them into a fine powder and put them into an egg-timer."
Herald Tribune, 23.3.79

Arthurian Legends

Responding to the complaints made by several of his parishioners after he had conducted a memorial service for a famous local drunkard, the Reverend James Owen of Cambridge said, "One is never surprised at a lack of charity".

During his memorial address, Dr Michael Avon said: "It is true that Arthur Mage was a homeless alcoholic who made well over 100 appearances before the bench. However, he once gave me the most perfect definition of Christian life — unfortunately it was some years ago and I have lost the piece of paper on which I jotted it down.

"Several times I met him when he was not hopelessly drunk and on each of these occasions we had very deep and profound conversations. Arthur was born to suffer. Often he was mugged for the money it had taken him days to beg."

The service was attended by representatives of the local Publicans Association, the police, Alcoholics Anonymous, and several uniformed ambulance workers.

The Reverend Owen said: "There are very good Christian reasons for this service, but I do not think it is proper to talk about them."
West Thames Gazette, 18.12.78

Cod's Wallop

"All my life my husband had dreamt of a giant catch," said Mrs Rhoda Head of Melbourne. "He was out fishing with my son Doug when he landed a 58lb cod. The shock killed him. After his funeral we had a fish supper: cod fritters on a bed of clams, with his name — Jerry Head — written in instant potato over the lot."
South China Morning Post, 31.10.78

Final Payment

"I was sitting in the car with my husband's ashes on my lap when Mr Perry approached me," said Mrs June Maltby of Vale.

"After looking through the window of the car and comparing my face with a photograph attached to the dossier he was carrying, Mr Perry knocked on the glass with his pipe and, when I wound down the window, he asked me for two weeks' rent.

"As a council tenant who has paid her rent regularly for over 47 years, I was furious. I explained to Mr Perry that I had been under sedation since my loss and this may have blurred my memory. He replied, 'Tell that to the computer'.

"It was then that I lost control of myself and threw my husband's casket into his face."

The Bucks Herald, 4.4.78

Cheap Burial

Mr Lemmy Chipowe, a magician of Chingola, Zambia, assured a small crowd that if anyone gave him one Zambian pound they could bury him alive for two and a half hours.

Mr M. Fitula, also of Chingola, gave him the money and helped to bury him.

Having waited for the time to elapse, the crowd dug him up. He was dead.

His wife said, "Something must have gone wrong."

A Zambian pound is worth 53 new pence.

Zambia Daily Mail, 7.8.72

Monumental Matrix

"It was while I was walking my dog in Pompano Beach Cemetery that I got the idea for Videostone," said Mr Donald Wells of Cheepie, Florida.

"I found the tombstones boring — always the same stuff, name, date of birth, ditto death, and that's all.

"When I got home I drew up the first plan for a power-operated audio-visual tombstone."

Mr Wells produced five prototype models. Each Videostone contained a film projector and a screen onto which films showing the deceased in typical scenes from his former life could be played.

"An important part of our marketing programme," said Mr Wells, "is to get prospective customers to open a tape and movie bank. When a customer thinks of something memorable to say he could come right down and we would film him in tasteful surroundings while he said it. We reckon to have full transmission within a week of the customer's last call."

Anon

Winning Ways

Should a passer-by have chosen to attend the funeral service of Mrs "Queen Bingo" Rose Worthy, an 88-year-old lady well-known in the Medway bingo parlours, he might have been surprised to hear Reverend Ellis open the service with the command: "Eyes up!"

"Having decided to speak the language of this particular congregation," said Rev. Ellis, "I changed the opening bingo cry of *eyes down* — for obvious reasons.

"Thereafter I reminded the mourners that it was God's intention to have a Full House, and that during the last Card Check everyone would discover that they were winners."

Sunday Express, 23.2.75

Long-term Parking

The President of Toyota Cars Ltd, octogenarian Mr Shotaro, has — at a cost of £168,000 — erected a shrine to commemorate the souls of those killed by and in his company's cars.

This road memorial covers 600 square feet and is made of blood-red concrete. It is sited among the pines of Tateshina, an exclusive mountain resort where senior members of Toyota Ltd often build summer fun-homes.
Sunday Telegraph, 2.8.70

Hot Potato

Preston District Council's Graves & Cemeteries Committee had second thoughts on its refusal of Mr Jack Morton's epitaph for his wife.

Her gravestone now reads: 'See you later, Spud'.
The Guardian, 28.8.75

Tennessee Schmaltz

Mr Raymond Ligon was appointed Chief Executive Manager of *Good Haven*, the first high-rise cemetery to be built.

"*Good Haven*", he said, "is a lavishly equipped mausoleum where people are free to come and pay their respects to the dead."

Standing at the junction of two important shopping centres in Nashville, Tennessee, the building is 20 storeys high, cost over twelve million dollars and will, when fully occupied, hold 135,000.

"We have made *Good Haven* a place that you really want to visit," Mr Ligon continued. "You will be able to have a non-alcoholic drink in a Garden of Jesus and pass on to a same-size reproduction of Christ's Tomb which incorporates stone from the Holy Land beneath a plexi-glass dome.

"It is no good being miserable about death. It is simply something that has got to be faced, like Watergate."

Rolling Stone, 22.11.73

Sutherland's Lore

A pre-recorded sermon tape was played through a speaker placed on the catafalque containing the earthly remains of Mr William Sutherland.

Eighteen months before his demise, Mr Sutherland, a retired headmaster, read his last words onto the tape.

"He lacked time for organised religion," said his son, William.

While she handed out copies of the Order of Service, stencilled by Mr Sutherland some weeks previously, Mrs Catherine Duncan said: "This event is absolutely typical of the man. He believed in doing everything himself."

The ceremony concluded with a recitation by Mr Sutherland of Bracken's *Not Understood*.

Aberdeen Press & Journal, 18.8.73

Cost of Inflation

Seeing what appeared to be a naked lady leaning from the window of a car and "waving for help", Constable John Harris gave chase and overhauled the vehicle.

In the car he found Mr George Floss of Banbury and a life-size inflatable doll "with breasts and other convincing attributes".

Mr Floss explained that as his wife had just left him four friends had clubbed together for the doll, "to cheer me up".

"After a few drinks," said Mr Floss, "I took a liking to the doll and decided to take her for a spin in the country."

He was fined £25 for having a dangerous load.

Evening Standard, 21.11.75

Judgement Day

After a series of complaints from his fellow lawmen, California Supreme Judge Marshall F. McComb was fired after 49 years service.

"Things have gone too far," said his colleague Judge Denver. "Hardly has Marshall hit the bench when he goes to sleep. Last week when I nudged him he shook himself awake and slipped out of the court: we thought he had gone to relieve nature but an usher told us he was placing a bet by telephone."

Asked to confirm that Judge McComb ate a green paper napkin instead of his salad, Mrs Darlene Jameson, the courthouse canteen manageress, said: "The Judge is always up to something unusual. He is a great favourite with the staff."
San Francisco Examiner, 11.7.76

Dutch Courage

Intending to rescue a man sitting on a pedallo four miles from the coast, Constable John Latham put to sea from Margate wearing his helmet and carrying his truncheon.

Reaching the pedalo and inviting the man into his dinghy, Constable Latham heard him cry, "I'm off to Amsterdam!"

After being hit on the head with a bottle, Constable Latham summoned the Margate lifeboat. The lifeboat set out with a crew of five, plus five more constables.

Four hours later the man, having knocked two lifeboat men overboard, was carried ashore handcuffed and lashed to a stretcher.

He did not give his name.
Daily Telegraph, 20.7.76

Peace Movement

Seventy-eight-year-old Mrs Elizabeth McClelland left Belfast, Ulster and went to Christchurch, New Zealand in order to avoid street violence.

Two years later she died in a Christchurch hospital after being hit over the head with an Irish civil rights placard during a demonstration.
Birmingham Post, 8.2.72

Duel Highwaymen

After Field Marshal Liber Serenge of the Uruguayan Army called General Juan Ribas, 77, of the same force "a socialist", they decided to fight a duel.

Meeting at dawn in Montevideo's Peoples' Peace Park, the two soldiers fired 137 rounds at each other from a distance of twenty-five paces. Neither man was hurt.

Sources close to General Ribas said that he aimed high on account of his opponent's advanced age and, in any case, "both refused to wear their glasses out of dignity".

Duelling is legal in Uruguay provided that the contestants are registered as blood donors.
New York Times, 28.12.71

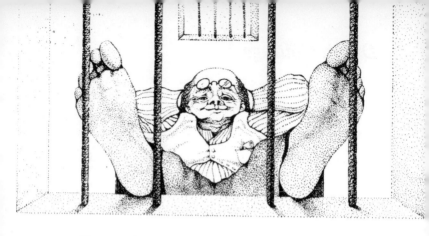

Stretching It

Shortly after refusing to pay 47p for the breakfast he had consumed in a Birmingham cafe, Mr Francis Whelan, an 86-year-old pensioner, was arrested.

The next day he refused to be released.

"Anyone who has to struggle along on a pension would be mad to leave Winson Green Prison," he said. "It's a real treat. Three square meals a day, central heating and plenty of new faces."

Mr Whelan rejected bail and remained in prison for three months.

"His is a unique case," said Mr Sime, the Recorder. "In all my experience I have never heard of the prosecution applying for bail on the part of the accused."

"I was hoping to stay in for Christmas," Mr Whelan said. "They say it's very, very good. Unfortunately I'll just have to find a room somewhere."

Mr Whelan's incarceration cost nearly £400.

"Why should I worry about the taxpayer?" he said. "I fought in two wars and worked all my life. If I'm not a taxpayer, who is?"

Mr Whelan was described by a social worker as "both rational and intelligent".

News of the World, 12.12.71

Dying Words

The Democratic Represen-
tative for New York State, Mr
John Rooney, said that Miss
Bernadette Devlin should not
be allowed into the United
States because "the last time
she was here my friend Mike
Dowd was so moved by her
eloquence he died of a heart
attack while listening to her."
Daily Telegraph

Chocolate-coated Cherry

Informed by his legal advisors that his defence against a charge of libel was worthless, Mr John Cherry, editor and publisher of the *Seattle Times*, agreed that the plaintiff, Mrs Diana Line, instead of receiving damages of £400 should be allowed to pelt him with custard pies.

On the appointed day, Mr Cherry stood on the steps of the Times building clad in a bathing suit and a skin-diver's helmet.

Because there were no custard pies available in Seattle, Mrs Line, accompanied by her two sons Fed (12) and Red (9), threw giant chocolate creams topped with Whippy Dip at the editor until his skin was coated.

Lawyer Ed MacGarry said: "I have had clients who got more money, but none who got greater satisfaction."
Manchester Evening News, 8.6.74

Stiff Joint

Customs officials at Cairo Airport discovered the director of a company that makes rosaries with 16lb of hashish stuffed in his artificial leg.
Daily Express, 13.10.71

The Fine Line

Emerging from the courtroom where he had just accepted a fine of some £18 for using a car without a current road licence, Mr Michael Wallis noticed another car whose licence had expired. It belonged to Mr Craven-Smith Willes, the magistrate who had just imposed the fine.
Daily Express, 11.7.70

Brothel Creeper

Soon after Sheriff Powell arrested 800 men during a raid on a famous South Carolina brothel, his office was inundated with telephone calls from those responsible, asking for their names to be removed from the charge-list.

Among the calls was one from an elderly man who offered $100 to have his name added to the list.

Daily Telegraph, 11.1.71

Life of Brian

The Jerusalem police prevented a Frenchman from crucifying himself on a hill just outside the town.

"There is no room for stunts like that around here nowadays," said a police spokesman.

The martyr said: "I have had myself crucified in seventeen different countries. I think it is a disgrace that it should be stopped in the place of its origin."

Daily Mirror, 3.4.70

MATRIMONY

Bats in the Belfry?

Mr Ronald 'Spook' Dickson, a popular singer with an ensemble called 'Nightmare', attended his wedding dressed as Count Dracula.

Driven to the Wolverhampton Registrar's Office in a hearse, Mr Dickson was carried to the office in a coffin by four of his fellow musicians dressed in green dayglo shrouds.

His bride was Miss Jacqueline Stamp, a 22-year-old professional dummy whom Mr Dickson met while he was hanging her as part of a musical entertainment.

The ceremony was attended by about 60 guests dressed as nuns, Vikings, members of MI5, cowboys and werewolves.

Glasgow Herald, 23.10.79

Driven to It. . .

"I was patrolling Redcliffe Parade," said Sergeant O'Duffy of the Brisbane Traffic Police, "when I saw the accused driving a souped-up wheelchair in an erratic manner. I signalled to him to stop but he revved up and began to weave in and out of the street furniture. Finally he went out of control and crashed into Standyman's Funeral Parlour."

Mr Drucy Jones (86) of Brisbane admitted to being drunk in charge of a wheelchair. "I had been visiting my ex-wife," he said. "We had our customary scene and I wanted to get away from her as quickly as possible."

Canberra Times, 8.9.79

Marriage Lions

During one of the fastest marriage ceremonies on record, Miss Julie Filipetto married Mr Gordon East in 15 seconds.

The ceremony took place in a cage and was watched by six wild lions.

The Minister, Mr Serge Whizzen of Detroit, had offered a free marriage to any couple "prepared to come together in the face of living nature".

Liverpool Echo, April 1978

Decree Absolute

While settling the details of their legal separation in the courtroom of Jacksonville, Florida, Mr and Mrs Rudell Hickson became involved in an argument.

Both parties pulled guns and shot it out from opposite ends of the judge's conference chamber.

Alarmed by this disruption of procedure, Mr Fred Lamp, who was giving evidence in an adjoining room, borrowed a pistol from Judge Everett Richardson and shot them both dead.

Washington Post, 23.12.72

Wedding Nerves

Relatives and friends attending the wedding of Miss Bindi Sha to Mr Hakim Nid were surprised to see the bride turn to her father-in-law-to-be and fracture his skull with a bottle of whisky.

Mr Nid Senior had not lost consciousness before Miss Sha butted his maiden sister in the stomach, put a half-nelson on her own father, Mr Ali Sha, and locked her mother into the temple lavatory.

Once in the street, Miss Sha stole her fiance's car, crashed it, and fled away through the crowd.

Later, the bridegroom said: "This is the first time Bindi has expressed any emotion towards me."

Kayham International, 9.10.73

Where There's A Will. . .

Miss Naomi Nicely of Greensburg, Pennsylvania asked the Westmorland Court to declare her to be an "official widow".

Miss Nicely and/or Mrs Neiderhiser was standing at the altar rails with Robert, her husband-to-be, when, in the middle of the ceremony, he dropped dead.

Giving evidence on behalf of Miss Nicely, the Rev. Captain Rag of Fort Palmer Unitarian Mission said: "Mr Neiderhiser fell to the floor as he uttered the binding words, 'I do'. As I bent over him he whispered, 'My God — I do', whereupon he died. The ceremony was over."
Daily Telegraph, 28.1.77

Sacre Bleu!

During his second trial for wife-murder, Mr Noel Carriou of Paris, France admitted that he killed his first wife because she undercooked his steak, and his second, twelve years later, because hers were always overdone.

Clearing him of murder but imposing an eight-year sentence for womanslaughter, Judge Filou said: "The quality of the cooking is an important part of marriage."
Daily Mirror, 17.11.73

High Church

Above an audience of 5,000, and under the big top of Oklahoma City, the trapeze artists Don Martinez and Lucy Fanfan were married by Bishop Ezra Nero of the Landmark Spiritual Temple.

Bishop Nero, suspended 75 feet in the air, shouted out the vows to Mr Martinez and Miss Fanfan as they arced to and fro.

Sun, 25.3.72

Jurisprudence

Dismissing a prospective juror from his court at Santa Cruz, California, Judge Brauer said:

"This woman is my wife. She never pays any attention to what I say at home and I have no reason to believe that her behaviour in court would be any different."

Daily Telegraph, 19.1.78

Traditional Ceremony

Before a congregation of some 120, the Reverend Clifford Lacey of St John's, Eltham began the nuptials of Rosemary Nicholson and David Mullett — a former choirboy.

The words "Dearly Beloved. . . " had scarcely passed the Rev. Lacey's lips when the bride's brother nipped out from behind the pulpit and panned across the faithful with his cine-camera, finishing the shot with a close-up of the verger, George Tubby, aged 72, a veteran of two world wars.

Rev. Lacey told Mr Nicholson to clear off; Mr Nicholson refused; whereupon, to the amazement of the devout, a shouting match developed between them, to which Mr Harry Nicholson, the bride's father, soon added his voice.

Rev. Lacey said that he had not given permission to photograph the choirgirls.

Leading schoolgirl Anne Butterbub said: "I feel sorry for the happy couple."

"Get on with it," said the bride's father. "He's not using lights."

Towards the end of the ceremony a bagpiper dressed in a kilt walked down the aisle, playing *Amazing Grace*. This disturbed the organist, Mr Beam, who played the theme from *Dr Zhivago* (the bride's personal request) all the louder.

Later, in the vestry, there was, according to the Vicar, "some jostling".

The bride's father, a retired paratrooper, said: "If the Queen can have her wedding on film, so can Rosemary" — and challenged the Reverend Lacey to a fight. Several wedding guests began to dance among the graves, and when Mr Tubby thrust his offertory plate towards them it was knocked into the air.

"The bagpiper is a relative," shouted Mr Nicholson. "This do cost me a tenner, and I've thrown it away."

Mr Tubby said, "I've done a couple of hundred of these in the last few months, but this one beats the lot. I was abused by the majority of the guests and all I got for the job was 50p."

Mr Nicholson, the bride's father, wrote a letter of complaint to the Archbishop of Canterbury.
Sunday Express, 4.6.72

Chief Barker

Writing to the "Ann Landers" agony column of the Toronto Daily Star, *a Canadian housewife complained that her daughter's husband-to-be, Courtney, had decided to have his dog Blaze as best man at the wedding.*

"Why be a hypocrite?" Courtney asked. "Blaze is my best friend."

Courtney is training Blaze to hold the ring in his mouth and to drop it into his master's hand when so ordered.

"My husband and I have agreed to attend the ceremony," the lady concluded, "but we are not going to pay for anything."
Toronto Daily Star, 10.3.69

The Bride Wore Goggles

Mr Arturo Sentora and Miss Barbara Durante were married on the seabed of San Frutuoso Bay, near Genoa.

"We are both diving enthusiasts," said Mr Sentora. "We provided the necessary equipment for Father Vogole, four witnesses and my best man. The bride carried a coral bouquet."

Guardian, 30.10.73

Flying Start

During his marriage ceremony at Conway, Mr Harry Vale, a local fashion photographer, was surprised when his wife-to-be gave birth to a baby boy in the pew to which he and his best man carried her.

"It was the first I had heard of it," said Mr Vale. "But Dora is an assistant nurse so she knew exactly what to do. When it was all over we carried on with the wedding as if nothing had happened."

The Daily Record, 22.8.78

Bum Rap

On the day before her divorce, Mrs Ursula Becker of Dortmund called at her husband's office to discuss the settlement of their property. In the course of her visit Mr Becker argued against their separation, but in vain. However, when the Judge asked her to tell the court how long it had been since they made love, Mrs Becker was surprised to hear her husband shout, "It's a lie!" when she said, "At least 18 months ago".

"We made love on the floor of my office yesterday morning!" yelled Mr Becker.

"He's the one who is lying!" shouted his wife.

"I can prove it," Mr Becker continued. "I marked her arse with the office date-stamp."

Mrs Becker's petition was rejected. *People, 15.3.70*

Constance Spry

After his singing had failed to win a prize at a local talent contest, Mr Edward Barefoot was assaulted by his wife, Constance.

"I had great hope in him," said Mrs Barefoot. "It was a 'Go As You Please' contest and I made him promise to sing *Happy-Go-Lucky Me* — one of our favourites. But when he reached the microphone he insisted on singing *Mon Amour* — in French. Needless to say, nobody present liked that sort of thing. So when he came back to his seat I hit him over the head with a hammer."
Newcastle Journal, 22.8.78

Ducking the Issue

Mr Milutin Velkjovic, an electrician from Belgrade, broke the world record for staying underground. Accompanied by a pair of Canadian ducks he remained below for 463 days. During this period his wife divorced him.
Daily Telegraph, July 1970

Wedding Bans

Miss Cheryl Blabury of Marjoram Close, Oxford was refused permission to have Mitzi, her chihuahua, as one of her bridesmaids.

Mitzi was to have been dressed in orange panties and a floral bonnet.
Yorkshire Post, December 1975

Egg On Her Face

Answering a knock at the front door of her home in Brighthouse, Yorkshire, Mrs Mavis Egg was astounded to see her husband, Harry, who had been officially listed as missing for the last four years after a skin-diving holiday in Whitley Bay.

"We had an argument about where he had been and I had to ask him to take his flippers off the kitchen table," she said. "Then he went upstairs and packed. We had a cup of tea and he went off saying that he would see me later."

A police spokesman said that Mr Egg had been struck off the missing persons list.

Daily Telegraph, 18.5.74

Grand Scales

"He has always been a favourite of mine — so I wanted him there on my big day," said Miss Geraldine Bateman, explaining the presence of Karl, a 16-foot Indian python that formed an archway under which she and her bridegroom, Mr Nicholas Ordinans, keeper of the giraffes at Worcestershire Zoo, passed after their marriage. Miss Bateman is an ape-house keeper at the same zoo.
Irish Times, 2.10.70

Fall Guy, Call Guy

"I admit I married my wife because she was a weight-lifter and after we had enjoyed ourselves she said she would beat me up unless I became her husband, but I received a profound shock when I discovered that she was also a prostitute," said Mr Robert Michaels of Exeter.

"Two days after we were married I came home after drawing my social security and found the house full of Hell's Angels.

"My wife told me to wait in the kitchen until she had finished work. After a few minutes she came into the kitchen in tears. She said that one of the Hell's Angels had left the house in disgust as soon as she took her clothes off. When I tried to cheer her up she turned nasty and insisted that I become a prostitute too.

"It took me a few weeks to get into the job. But the charge that I am living off my wife's immoral earnings is quite untrue. We pool what we earn. It comes to about £9 a week, plus the security, and this is not enough to satisfy her longing for expensive clothes.

"We are both very unhappy, but we have decided to make a go of it."

Southern Evening Echo, 1.11.79

MEDICAL

Gone With The Wind

An Irishman, an aristocrat and a true eccentric, developed a new obsession.

Driving through the countryside, he stopped his car beside some men of honest toil. They were opening up the road.

"Good morning," said the Peer. "May I borrow your hammer, please?" Given the hammer, he smashed his windscreen to smithereens, returned the tool to its rightful owner and drove off, declaring, "Wind resistance — it is the cause of all Ireland's troubles."

Later that week he was playing golf with a group of men and women hardly less elevated than himself. Throughout the game he was explaining his wind-resistance theory. When they reached the seventh tee he could bear inactivity no longer. To free himself of unnecessary restriction he stripped naked and thus completed the game.

None of his companions commented.

Anon

Diet and Die

Dr Alice Chase, the author of Nutrition for Health *and several other works on clean living, died of malnutrition.*
Daily Mail, 28.4.73

Navel Rating

"I was completely satisfied by the way Mr Dearing remodelled my breasts," said Miss Claude Hankin of Nettlefold, Indiana. "When he suggested that I should have a new navel I fell in with his plans. But it is not the sort of navel I want.

"In the first place it is eight inches above the site of my old navel. Mr Dearing assured me that the navel he intended to create would resemble a small walnut. I have finished up with something more like a coconut."

Mr Dearing said that he had done his best to construct a walnut effect but that Miss Hankin's tissues were less than first-class material.

After the failure of the operation he had offered to marry her but she had declined his offer.
New York Times, 5.10.77

Cold Comfort

Impatient with the monotony of his life, Mr Joseph Harrod, a retired lock-keeper of Newark, Nottinghamshire, decided to kill himself.

In the space of 24 hours he tried self-electrocution twice, twice cut his throat, and drank one and a quarter bottles of whisky.

Surviving these efforts, he died of a bad cold four days later.

Daily Express, 14.1.74

Paper Tigress

"I resisted the habit while I was in training, but after my marriage the craving returned and I surrendered to temptation," said Nurse Jane Wilmot.

Nurse Wilmot faced a medical enquiry after it was alleged that she had eaten 35 birth certificates, the property of the maternity home where she was once employed.

"As a schoolgirl I used to consume blotting paper and this escalated to exercise books," she said. "By the time I left school I was lunching off a small packet of tissues and the front page of the *Melbourne Times*.

"In my first job I found that a diet of luncheon vouchers and bus tickets suited me best," Nurse Wilmot continued. "However, I lost my boyfriend over it; and at that point I decided to become a nurse. Everything went well until I married."

Evening Standard, 18.9.76

Slow Death

The oldest man in Alabama, Mr Hercules Golightly, died at the age of 121. His wife said:
"He had been poorly since he fell out of a tree while gathering nuts on his 111th birthday."
Daily Mail, 20.11.71

Current Movements

Having a patient who had been constipated for 40 days, Dr A. Cabe of Lyons introduced the negative pole of a Gaiffe battery to the lady's rectum and applied the positive pole to her navel.

"Two minutes later we had a satisfactory movement," he said.
Scientific American, August 1970

Iron Constitution

A man, Milivoja Ristic, 76, a Serbian from Bor, has bought a derelict bus which he plans to eat over a period of two years.

Mr Ristic has already consumed 22,500 razor blades, two and a half hundredweight of glass, eight pounds of lead shot and a jeep.

"I've always been like this," he said. "During the war I ate ordinary food but it ruined my stomach."
Sunday Express, 14.12.69

A Date a Day

A group of anthropologists investigating the lives of tribesmen in the Aleg region of Mauritania discovered the oldest woman alive. She is aged 170 years, and has 300 grandchildren spread over seven generations — some of whom are well over the 100 mark themselves.

"The lady", their report stated, "is completely senile. Nevertheless, she manages to eat 12 pounds of dates a day."
Evening News, 20.7.70

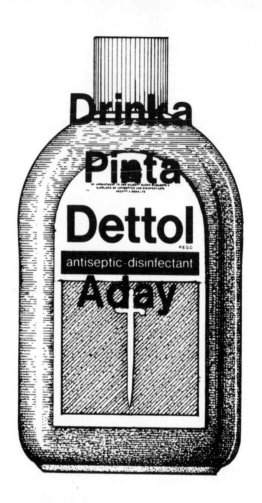

Germ Welfare

Sent to hospital for an overall service, Mrs Ellen Lesley, a toothbrush examiner, admitted that she had been a Dettoloholic for eleven years.

"I drink about a pint a day," she said.

Extensive testing revealed that Mrs Lesley's liver and kidneys were in tip-top shape.
Daily Mirror, 24.3.79

To Be Sniffed At

Interviewed at his Bombay luxury home, Mr Jagdish Morarji, a prominent Indian urinobibe, said: "I possess irresistible medical statistics to prove that rhinoceros urine is a cure for the common cold. It was the British who crushed our natural ayurvedic health system. People say that I am a Hindu fanatic. This is nonsense. I drink brandy and smoke several cigarettes a year. Every Indian family should keep a bowl of urine, preferably very old urine, on the kitchen shelf. Urine knows no religion. Why, only the other day, when I was flying from Calcutta to Delhi, I engaged a fellow passenger in conversation. He turned out to be C. Szent Gyorgagee, India's Poet Laureate, who was suffering from English Flu. He took a deep swig from my bottle of Rhinorine and by the time we landed he was cured. What further evidence is needed to show that my treatment is the only treatment? Fill up and feel the difference!"
The Bombay Standard, 1.10.78

Starlight Flit

"I had been suffering from dizzy spells," said raven-haired Mrs Gwendolyn Charger of Stamford Place, Felixstowe, "so I decided to visit Madame Starlight, our local metahealth expert.

"On my first visit she asked me to pull up my woolly and rubbed tomato juice into my skin for about an hour. Because I felt a good deal better, I did as Madame Starlight said and two days later I returned with £50 in my purse, which she said she would bless.

"Having handed her the purse she would not return it to me, and in our struggle her wig fell off and I saw that she was a man.

"I went home to fetch my husband and when we returned to the consulting room there was a notice on the door saying: *Have gone to the Holy Land*."
Bedfordshire Times, 28.7.78

Mean Difference

As head of the Department of Psychiatry at Asfahan University, Persia, Dr Biktami was in demand as an expert opinion witness for the prosecution in all major criminal trials.

Finding himself in the dock accused of stealing 1,067 chairs, over 178,000 rubber bands, 959 desks, 340 typewriters, 73 microscopes, 14,000 ball-point pens and 754 yards of industrial lino, Dr Biktami remained loyal to authority and gave an expert opinion of himself:

"I am a distinguished kleptomaniac," he said. "Kleptomania is a medical disorder which demands careful treatment rather than incarceration."

The judge was about to order his release when the prosecution offered a different opinion of kleptomania given by Dr Biktami in the same court earlier in his career.

"Kleptomania," the doctor had said, "is a mean type of theft and should be vigorously punished."

He got six months.
Daily Mail, June 1968

Fairy Tales

After she had complained of deafness, a tooth, carefully wrapped in tissue paper, was removed from the ear of Mrs Muriel Diceu, 96, of Cardiff.

"I must have put it on my pillow in 1895 hoping that the fairies would bring me sixpence. I have often wondered what became of it and now the mystery is solved."
Daily Telegraph, 28.8.79

PERSONAL

A Gun For Sale

Mr Eric Mayton (92) and his wife Dolly (91) decided on a joint suicide.

However their instrument, an 1884 pearl-handled ·22 garter pistol, let them down.

Its first shot glanced off one of Mrs Mayton's hair-curlers and the second, aimed by Mr Mayton at his own head, only lodged in his ear.

Concussed but hale, resting in an adjacent bed to his wife at Vancouver General Hospital, Mr Mayton said:

"We have decided to see the matter out naturally."

Jersey Evening Post, 4.7.75

Dish of the Day

Feeling a bit peckish, Mr Jack Sellick entered a restaurant close to the Severn Bridge, settled his twenty-six stones behind a table, and ordered a large plateful of sausages and mash.

Having demolished the meal, Mr Sellick wished to be on his way. However, the table was bolted to the floor and the bench on which he was sitting was fixed to the wall by similar contrivances, both of which prevented him, newly distended, from rising.

A discreet conversation with the proprietor revealed Mr Sellick's predicament.

Four useful workmen were called; after forty minutes of intense spanner and screwdriver work Mr Sellick's 58-inch girth could move freely.

"I nearly died of shame," he said, "but the other customers just went on eating and ignored it all."

Anon

Blind Spot

While queuing for his supper in the Pisces Midnite Fishery, Horndean, Mr Henry Foster felt the need to blow his nose. As he did so, his glass eye shot from its socket and landed in the deep-fry chip tank.

When Mr John Fratton, the Fishery's manager, announced that service would be discontinued until the tank had been drained and cleaned, several of his customers became restive.

"It was as much a shock to me as it was to him," said Mr Foster. "I kept my head until he removed the eye with a pair of tongs and threw it across the counter onto the Fishery's floor. Then I saw red, reached across the counter and slapped his face."

Somerset County Gazette, July 1977

To Witte, a Daughter

"I am not a wealthy man,"
said Arthur Fisher of Bogside,
"so I had my daughter
registered at birth as Charlotte
Maria Elisabeth Keith de Witte-
Scott-Fisher, Viscountess de
Witte, in order to give her a
fair start in life."
Daily Mail

Behind Closed Jaws

Having inserted one end of a plastic sack through the letterbox at No. 16 Tiddley Mews, Buckthorpe, dustman George Stevenson sensed that it had been grabbed "in a strange way" and, "in spite of the fact that I was delivering it", held on to his own end. When the sack was again jerked forward, Mr Stevenson hauled it back towards him and "held on for dear life".

"My strength was about to go," he said, "so I called my mate and we hung on together."

"I took a good grip of the sack," said Mr David Lifer, "and as soon as the inside puller relaxed we gave a big heave. The front door came away from its hinges and fell on top of us. Clinging to the far end of the sack we saw a crocodile."

Adjourning the case for "further investigation", the magistrate, Mr Douglas Brody, said: "The tenant's pet crocodile 'Jaws' had been trained to carry the morning paper upstairs."

The Times, 21.2.76

Boa Constricted

Senhor Michaelangeli Phuta of Belem, Brazil was arrested for entering a cinema with Dolores, his pet boa constrictor, around his neck. Senhor Kaukmann, manager of El Stella, Belem's only cinema, said: "The snake was under age."

Senhor Phuta said: "Dolores goes where I go. We had been looking forward to seeing *Gone With The Wind* for six years."

The Sun, 23.2.72

Monkey Business

"The new law seriously infringes my fundamental liberties as an adult male Iranian taxpayer", said Mr Heydar Qassemi, "and I consider it my duty to uphold those liberties."

Mr Qassemi was answering a charge of wife-beating; not by himself, but by his pet monkey Makmal the Third.

"For upwards of seventeen years I have given my wife a good beating on the last Tuesday of every month. When the new law against this ancient right was passed I taught Makmal to do the job instead. It was not my intention that he should knock out my wife's gold tooth, but you cannot get everything right first time."

"Makmal has always taken Heydar's part in our monthly quarrels", said Mrs Tajmah Qassemi, "just like his father and grandfather before him — but none of them went as far."

Mr Qassemi was sentenced to three months' imprisonment. He was allowed to take Makmal to prison with him.
Sun, 5.6.73

Bird Calls

"I was watching the news in the sun-lounge when a budgerigar flew in through the window and landed on the indoor aerial," said Miss Mary Tanner of Ware. "I extended my finger to the bird. He hopped onto it and said, "443701", which I instantly recognised as his telephonic address. His owners drove over to pick him up later in the day."
The Scotsman, 18.5.77

Final Nesting Place

Thinking that the time had come to give her budgie's cage a good clean, Mrs Hazel Dawson of Witton Gilbert, Durham decided to use her vacuum cleaner.

"I switched it on and whoosh! . . . one moment Beauty was chirping away, the next all I could see were tufts sticking out of the nozzle. When I pulled them, they just came away in my hands."
Daily Express, 2.5.72

Snake Bite

"I was taking Mr Slippy, my python, for his usual rideabout," said Naomi Anderson of Morganton, North Carolina, "when we were halted at the intersection of Jackson and Atlantic and Mr Surling pulled up alongside.

"As usual, Mr Slippy had his tail stuck out of the nearside window and when Mr Surling asked if he could touch it I said he could. Whereupon he grabbed Mr Slippy's tail and bit an inch off. Then he spat it out, laughed, and drove away."

Asked why he had bitten the python, Mr Surling replied, "I am a jazz drummer. I must be free."

He was fined $500.

Rome Daily American, 27.4.78

Law of the Jungle

Eight lurking policemen pounced on Mr David Gore as he approached the ransom point at which he had agreed to deliver 'Aggie', a golden parrot, to Mrs Winifred Pascoe, a Cornish pet-dealer.

"I kidnapped Aggie", he said, "in order to obtain compensation for the pair of fan-tailed goldfish I bought from Mrs Pascoe last year.

"When I found them floating on the surface of the water and took them back, Mrs Pascoe told me to buy a cat and feed them to it."

Daily Telegraph, 12.3.76

Nap of the Day

Mr Philip Davis of Farnham, Surrey owned a gelding called Rodger who was in the habit of sleeping on his back with his legs in the air, eyes shut and mouth open.

This attitude caused so many motorists to telephone the local police that Mr Davis erected a large sign in Rodger's field saying 'THIS HORSE IS NOT DEAD'.

Daily Mirror, 1.7.71

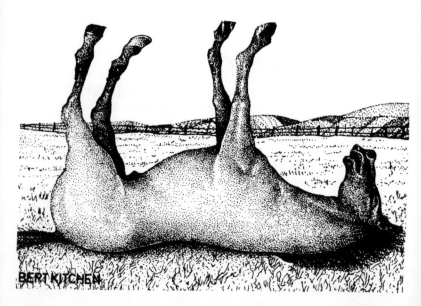

BERT KITCHEN

POLICE

Bin End

Herr Wolfgang Murstein, a barber of Dusseldorf wanted by the police for eating numerous substantial meals in West German restaurants and then sneaking off without paying, was arrested while lying in the waste-bin of a fashionable Friburg dinery.

The cook, Dr Horst Tizer, said: "We served Herr Murstein three large platters of cold ham, followed by a roast knuckle of pork. When the waiter approached with the bill, he dashed through the kitchens and fell into the swill."

However, before he could be charged he died of gluttony.

International Herald Tribune, 27.10.75

Californian Rope Trick

The Chief of the Los Angeles Police, Mr Edward Davis, perfected a lightweight portable gallows for punishing hijackers.

"My idea is simple and traditional," said Chief Davis. "We have a moving courtroom in a bus and the gallows is towed behind it in a small trailer. As soon as the criminal is grabbed, we hold a quick trial, find him guilty, and hang him on the main runway right beneath the observation platform. My gallows has a titanium crossbar and a nylon rope — the trap is fully automatic. All I am waiting for is the re-introduction of the death penalty."

Sun, 4.8.72

Fine Performance

Five minutes after half-time Mr Kenneth Roberts, playing as a forward for Hoylake in their match against the Liverpool Police XV, found himself being arrested on the field.

"The fact that the police were losing plus the fact that Mr Roberts had been a prominent scorer against them had nothing whatsoever to do with this arrest," said a police spokesman.

"I would like to make it perfectly clear to everyone", said Mr Roberts, "that the offence for which I was arrested was the non-, or rather the merely delayed, payment of a parking fine."

"Several matters became intertwined," said the spokesperson.

Daily Telegraph, 23.4.76

Murder by Degrees?

Admitting that Mr Robert Wilson had escaped from their custody while he was being charged with killing Mr Henry Peter, the Garda press office said, "He is no more dangerous than any other murderer."
The Sunday Independent, 4.4.78

Sights Unseen

After an intensive but fruitless search for a negative precedent, the police of Ecorse, Michigan issued a gun permit to a blind man.
Herald Tribune, 5.2.71

POLITICS

Poll Cats

Mr Douglas Mist, a paper merchant of Southend, was summoned under sections 22 and 70 of the People's Regulations for giving false information to his local Registration Officer in that he caused the names of his two cats, Ginger Mist and Tiny Tim Mist, to be inscribed on the electoral register.

In his defence Mr Mist said that his cats were British subjects, that they were both over 21, would be inheriting his house when he died, and as house-holders they were entitled to a vote.
Daily Telegraph, 1961

Bloomer Rumour

Wife-swapping is commonplace in Basildon, said the prospective Liberal candidate, Mr Stanley Balls.

"There aren't enough amenities here," he said. "My wife goes out to work so she has something to stimulate her mind."

The Conservative candidate, Mr Tony Ball, said: "I don't think our town is worse than any other."

Liberal Balls replied: "If he doesn't know what's going on he has no right to represent the people.

Asked to produce evidence or apologise, Balls said: "I was repeating a rumour I heard five years ago about Ilford."
Morning Star

A Swansong for Europe?

Professor James Double, a social historian, revealed that by 1.30pm of the day of the elections for the European Parliament only one ballot paper had been completed in the South Birmingham constituency.

"The voter's name was Mrs Grizzle, an 83-year-old secretary," he said. "Mrs Grizzle did not think her vote would help England because 'Israel has already won'.

"Mrs Grizzle thought she was voting in the Eurovision Song Contest. She was carrying a copy of the *Radio Times*, opened at the voting page."
Birmingham Evening Mail, 11.7.79

Lord of the Flies

During his interview Lord Russell, the philosopher's son, agreed that he had admonished the House of Lords.

"It is a Marxist institution," he said, "and I am their dissident."

Interrupted by howling aristocrats in the middle of a speech recommending the total abolition of law and order as the only way to stop "youngsters being raped by policemen", he advocated the replacement of the Force by members of the Salvation Army.

"Let women have as many husbands as they want," he continued, "and make the automation of all work compulsory."

Asked if the self-crocheted pair of trousers he was wearing were among the kinds of manufactured article suitable for automated production, His Lordship said: "It would be a very, very difficult programme to compose. While they were being made I had to keep taking them off because there was no pattern."
Warrington Guardian, 23.6.78

Shit Hot

The Republican Governor of Oklahoma, David Hall, surrendered his title of world champion shit-thrower to former Governor Dewy Bartlett at Beaver, Oklahoma.

Before an audience estimated by the State Police to be well over 15,000, the two politicians — each standing before a tub of cowshit — took off their jackets and hurled hand-sized pats towards a white-washed target.

Governor Hall, who managed 94 feet the previous year, could do no better than 68 feet. But former Governor Bartlett managed 138 feet.

"It was a fair contest," said Hall, "and the best man won. The weather was ideal for the occasion. Warm, lots of sunshine, with a light breeze to give the pat that added zip."
Montreal Sunday Express, 23.4.72

Silent Knight

Rising in the House of Lords, Thomas Coke — The Earl of Leicester — said that it was the first time in 22 years he had made a speech. Public silence was traditional in the Coke family, he said. His father never made a speech in his 23 years as a member of the House; nor his grandfather in his 32-year membership; nor his great-grandfather during 67 years of regular attendance.

The Earl spoke on pollution. He said he thought it was a bad thing.
Daily Telegraph, 18.4.72

Lolly Polly!

After the Prime Minister of Australia, one Mr McMahon, had been pelted with jelly-babies in the town of Perth, secret service agents collected the evidence, arrested fifteen assorted rowdies and, prior to charging them, returned to guard their leader while he addressed a crowd of several thousand voters.

When everyone had gone home they returned to base and released their catch.

"We could bring no charges," said a secret service spokesman, "because the evidence had been eaten by Bozo, a cockatoo."

Melbourne Age, 7.11.72

Dead Cert

Describing the occasion as "a bad mistake", Mr Phil Wran, the town clerk of Burwood, Australia, apologised to the 8,731 people who voted to have George Sims as their mayor.

"We had no idea at the time the ballots were issued that Mr Sims was dead.

"When it was announced that he had been re-elected there was an outcry."

"This is too bad," said Mrs Audrey Jenkins, sister-in-law of the deceased. "George was very popular among the townsfolk. Imagine my surprise when, after returning from the cremation, I heard his election victory being announced on the Western Australian radio."
Sydney Morning Herald, 2.6.74

Banana Split

Discontented with the administration of their village, the inhabitants of Moogue, West Mexico invaded the office of Mayor Ramon del Cueto, forced him to eat 12lbs of bananas, and made him sign a letter of resignation.
18.9.78

SCIENCE

Soul Survival

An eccentric Arizonan miner called James Kidd
vanished into the mountains of his native state,
never to be seen again. After some time he was
declared legally dead. His will provided two be-
quests: 1) $100 to "some preacher for saying
goodbye", and 2) a $200,000 residue "for research
into the existence of the human soul which leaves
the body at death".

The claimants to this money were numerous.
One of them, Mrs Higgins, a Californian medium,
said: "Mr Kidd appeared in my bedroom and
smiled at me. Then he changed into a fluorescent
light and went through the ceiling. I want to build
a lunatic asylum with the money."

Another claimant, Mr Ludwig Rosencrans, said
he wanted the money to publish a book proving
that the entire world population went mad in 1950.
Daily Mirror

Safety Tip

A field party from the International Association for Dental Research issued a report on the development of mouth cancer in smokers.

After an examination of 52 South American cigar-smokers they were able to show that those who smoke the cigar with the lighted end in their mouths are safe from the disease.

"We reached the conclusion that the temperature of 870° often generated in the mouths of reverse-smokers is in some way beneficial."
Anon, 1968

Aah! Condor!

Sitting on the porch of his farm house near Castelfranco Veneto, Stefano Marchetti, aged 80, was about to light his pipe when a bolt of lightning struck the bowl and did the job for him. Mr Marchetti continued undisturbed.
Sun, 2.6.71

Total Recoil

Sigrid Hemse from Gotland, Sweden planned to sue Mr Uri Geller, the conjuror, for unwanted pregnancy.

Miss Hemse claimed that her contraceptive device was distorted by Mr Geller while she and her husband-to-be, Mr Sven Malmo, were making love during his television show.

"My fiance and I often make love to television," she said, "and this has never happened before. I was not in a position to actually see the show, but I heard all about it afterwards from my mother who lives upstairs.

"I am convinced Mr Geller has unusual powers and I hope he recognises his responsibility for them."

Daily Telegraph

Hooked on Nails

Having grown his fingernails to an average length of eight inches and having spent over 12,000 rupees on nail polish in the past nine years, Mr Murari Mohan Adiya of Calcutta wrote to the *Guinness Book of Records*, soliciting inclusion.

"My glorious achievement represents no mere record," he said. "It is an object of wonder to all human beings — and in these good and democratic days it should be the right of every person in the free world to pay a small sum of money to behold these miraculous nails in International Exhibition.

"I drink not, neither do I smoke. My nails are the only intoxication I enjoy."

Daily Mail, 22.6.71

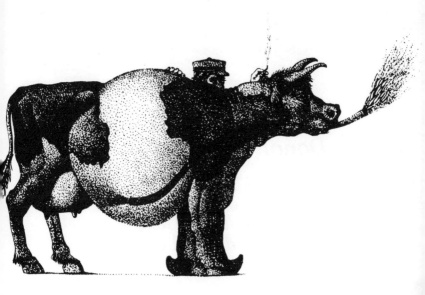

High Speed Gas

Called to the village of Lictenvoorde in Holland, Mr Jap Muooy was asked to treat 'Miss Utrecht', a prize cow so blown with flatulence that she had become almost three times her natural size.

"As is usual in such cases," said Mr Muooy, "I inserted a large hose through Miss Utrecht's mouth and when it reached her stomach applied a match to the free end. Much to my surprise, a flame roared forth which ignited the barn. In next to no time the farm was a pile of ash."

Anon

Donor's Delight

Mr Paul Santon, a 77-year-old caretaker of Toulouse, entered Toulouse General Hospital and asked the porter if he could donate his body to science.

On being told that he could, Mr Santon shot himself dead.
The Times, 2.2.76

SPORTING LIFE

Chicken Feed

Mr Bozo Miller was an eating champion. Around the age of nine he ate 40 hot-dogs to amuse his companions at a baseball game. Some fifty years later Mr Miller was still very competitive.

"Athletes?" he said, "They're peanuts. Height doesn't mean a thing. Take me — five seven, around 280 pounds. Take one of them — six seven or eight, maybe 300 pounds. OK. We start on steaks; after a dozen three-pounders they quit. If anyone's still with me I switch to ice cream sundaes, one, two dozen. . . after that I'd destroy him with hot sauces and minestrone. Fluids are my great strength."

Once Bozo won the toss for a championship contest held in the Starlite Lounge of San Francisco's Hilton. He chose chicken. In fifteen minutes he demolished twenty-seven two-pound pullets and picked up a purse of $10,000.

"I train for about two weeks," he said. "Each day I have my wife force-feed me with solids and fluids until I'm near bursting point. I reckon to put on about 25 pounds. The secret is — have an elastic sac.

"If your sac's elastic, if you have the necessary confidence, then there is only one thing that can beat you — speed. I'm speedy. Get it down fast. Get it down whole. Get it down first. The three goldens. Bang! I once finished 37 7-Ups before my opponent had downed four. He quit."

Bozo was allergic to snails and cream crackers. He would not eat them in competition.

"In 1942 I ate ten pounds of cream crackers. They nearly killed me. It took me eight weeks before I had a free movement."

New York Times, 2.5.68

An Eye for a Record

Herr Hermann Schnatz was declared World Champion snuff-taker after he reduced the global record for snuffing one-sixth of an ounce of 'Periwig Special' from 55 to 53.02 seconds.

During the event Mr Schnatz sneezed so violently that his glass eye shot across the mat and into the judge's box.

"We are quite used to this sort of thing," said Herr Karsk, the Championship organiser.

"Last year we had four lost dentures and a rupture."
Anon.

A Nose for Success

While setting a new Ferret-Down-Your-Trouser world record time, Mr Edward Simpkins of the Isle of Wight sustained two nasty bites. "He gritted his teeth", said his manager, "and continued playing a successful game of darts."

"We have applied for entry to the Olympics," said an Island spokesperson, "and I have no doubt that Ted will bring home a Gold. He doubled the existing time of 90 minutes to four hours. Then — after a short break — he went on to create a new Pairs record of two down for 70 minutes. It was fantastic."

Isle of Wight County Press, 8.1.77

My Cup Runneth Over. .

The secretary of an Irish football club asked his wife to take a presentation tankard to the engravers. The inscription "To M.P. Cosgrave in appreciation for the Whitsun 1971 Tour from the Ballsall Hornets" was duly placed on the tankard's side.

However, because the words had been written out on a shopping list, it continued: "One bottle of shoe cleaner and a pair of white laces".
International Herald Tribune, 25.5.71

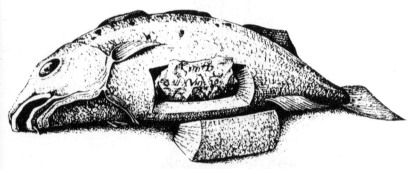

Cod's Woe

Mr Robin Chapman of East Dereham, Norfolk caught a 12-pound cod whose stomach contained a packet of salt and vinegar flavoured crisps.
Daily Express, 1.4.71

Touch-line Tactics

In Lima, Peru, a forty-minute football match refereed by Sister Soledad Vasquez resulted in a 2-2 draw. An unusual feature of this match was the fact that both teams were blind.

"They played", said Sister Vasquez (who was also their trainer), "with a ball which contained a handful of dried peas. In that way everybody knew where it was."

Reuter

Spectator Sport

Chronic adult misbehaviour stopped the football matches being played between Northamptonshire Scout troops.

"We did our best to ignore spectator rowdyism throughout the year," said Mr Croxley Hyssop, a Scout District Commissioner. "However, during the finals, a gang of parents began to fight each other at the touchline.

"Mr Gregory Post, a volunteer referee, had his shorts torn off; and matters came to a head when our linesman, Mr David Horner, who is obliged to use an invalid car, was chased across the pitch by two brawling mothers."

Asked if the six-year ban on Scout football was not too severe, Mr Hyssop replied: "I have blown the whistle for the last time."

Sunday Times, November 1977

Unanswered Prayer

The world-famous footballer, Roberto Rivelino, has increased his popularity by scoring the fastest goal on record in football history.

One second after the opening of a match in Bahia between Corinthians and Rio Preto, Mr Rivelino scored with a left-foot drive from the half-way line. The ball went past the ear of Isadore Irandir, Rio Preto's goalkeeper, while he was finishing his pre-match prayers in the goalmouth.

Before the match was resumed, Joachim, Mr Irandir's brother, ran onto the field, drew his revolver, and fired six shots into the ball.

As he was being led off he received an ovation from the good-natured crowd.

Evening Standard, 8.7.74

Galloping Dog

Mr Tom Wattle, a keen supporter of Chelsea football club, was fined £10 for sticking a hot-dog up the anus of a police horse called Eileen.

"I was overcome with excitement after the match," he said. "I wanted to get rid of the hot-dog and just at that moment Eileen wandered by. I intended no harm and am a genuine animal lover."
Fulham Chronicle, 5.11.76

Expert Angle

At Angers, France, a Mr Robert Expert landed a 15lb pike while taking part in an angling contest.

Exclaiming, "This is the biggest catch of my life!" Mr Expert dropped dead in front of his fellow competitors.
Evening Standard, 21.12.72

Novice's Handicap

Entered for the world's first worm race, Willy, a 12-inch British earthworm, was crushed by his trainer Mr Christopher Hudson of Hove, Sussex.

"I am very upset," said Mr Hudson. "Willy was a clear favourite. I was so excited by his prospects that I forgot he was behind me when I stepped back to answer a phone call confirming his entry."
Press & Journal, 18.1.71

Record Swim

Mr Gene Roberts, a legless Vietnam war veteran, abandoned his attempt to swim the Channel after two hours in the water. He was accompanied by Mr Richard Freeman, a blind advertising man from Banstead, Surrey. The pair navigated by listening to the sounds of a gramophone screwed to the transom of a preceding dinghy filled with friends and well-wishers.
BBC News, 5.9.71

Hole in One

A ball driven from the 10th tee of Quinindi golf course by Mr Robert Wilson struck a tree, penetrated the windscreen of a passing moped, and lodged in the driver's mouth.

Guardian, 17.6.71

Pip Squeaks

Discharged after their arrest for disorderly conduct at a football match, two 15-year-old boys explained: "We always throw oranges at our goalie."

The player in question, Ian McKechnie, goalkeeper for Hull, said: "I like oranges. It's a long-standing tradition with our club that the popular end pelt me with oranges during the game. On a good day I get as many as 30 juicy Jaffas."
Daily Mirror, 30.8.71

Irish Stew

One evening in November Mr John Dunne and his wife Nora were making their way home by the Liffey's quays. Twenty feet below them lay 15 feet of water. They fell in.

Following them down the quay was Nora's brother Mr Noel Dooley and his girlfriend Miss Colette O'Brien; no sooner had John and Nora Dunne hit the water than Noel and Colette dived to their rescue.

Unfortunately none of them could swim. Two policemen — O'Hara and Mulligan — hearing the four of them crying for help also dove in. Alas, they too were non-swimmers.

By this time a fair-sized crowd had gathered on the quay; shouts of encouragement and blame were directed to the drowning six, and two passers-by — Mr Johnny Byrne and Mr Brendan Behan — dove to their rescue.

Although both men were strong swimmers they were so weighed down with their rescuees that in next to no time they were drowning too.

Twenty feet above them, the crowd had grown larger. A man appeared with a loud-hailer to give advice; a woman seized it from him and reminded the drowners of their alcoholic ways; motorists shone their headlamps onto the water.

At last the fire brigade arrived. It took them 15 minutes to force their way through the crowd to the water's edge. They pulled the eight from the water — only the two strong swimmers, Byrne and Behan, were seriously hurt. The ambulance took them to hospital. The other six, including the two policemen — O'Hara and Mulligan — became involved in a long argument with the crowd.
Sunday Independent, 9.11.69

Protection Racket

"We cater to the armchair hunter," said Mr George McHugh, Chairman of the Florida Wildlife Association.

"All over the country there are zoos wanting to dispose of elderly lions, tigers, cougars and leopards. We pay them the going price, put the geriatric cats in a cage, and let people shoot them from chairs.

"At first we decided to let them out, but this was unpopular with both the animals and the hunters. The animals didn't want to run about and the hunters didn't want to chase them."

"Of course there have been complaints," said Captain Fish, the FWA's business manager, "but let's not be sentimental. These animals have reached the end of their useful lives. They are killed harmlessly and humanely. It gives pleasure to people."
South China Morning Post, 4.7.78

Argentinian Beef

Miss Collette Duveen, a nun belonging to the Order of Merciful Sisters, was arrested for kicking in the teeth of a truck driver who shouted 'Hooray!' when he saw Holland score their second World Cup goal against Argentina.
News of the World, 30.6.78

Pot Crack

Mr Robert Fairtree of Melbourne, a snooker enthusiast who wished to invent a new shot that would become known as 'a Fairtree', had himself suspended upside-down over the table with helium-filled balloons attached to his wrists and his legs fastened to the rafters.

While making his shot he fell head-first onto the cloth and died.
Hong Kong Standard, 2.1.79

Heavy Penalty

Mr Thomas Haycock, a goalkeeper, was dropped from the Greentown BME after their failure to win a match in four seasons of 'uphill football'.

"Haycock's game fell to pieces after the team began to call him 'Cheesecake'," said Mr Haston Lash, Greentown's manager. "I know that he weighs almost 20 stone and that top-of-the-net work upsets him. Nevertheless, he has let in 107 goals in three matches."

"Why blame me?" said Mr Haycock. "If the team worked together I would have nothing to do. Instead, they began to call me 'Cheesecake' when the ball was flashing around me. We were only losing 17-0 at half-time. They give up too easily."

Before leaving the clubhouse, Mr Haycock said that he had not given up hope and that he would do his utmost to get back into the team.

Yorkshire Post, 2.11.77

A Belly-full of It!

A shark weighing 457lbs was caught off Antigua. Its stomach contained one pair of two-tone suede beach boots, a human skull and a copy of the Gospel of St John printed on polythene.

Evening News, 15.5.72

Long Shot

Lady golfers enjoying the amenities of Kingarth Links,
Isle of Bute were startled when a torpedo streaked out of
the rough and came to rest on the first green.
It was collected by the Navy.
Daily Mirror, 22.7.70

TRANSPORT

Fare Cop

An Athenian taxi driver was surprised to be given his own address as his fare's destination. He was further surprised when the fare alighted and, producing a key, let himself into the driver's house.

This emotion was generalised when the driver, using his own key, disturbed his fare's and his wife's adultery.

"It must have been his unlucky day," said the driver. "Athens has 70,000 taxis."
Evening News, 13.11.70

Motorway Madness

The police asked an 85-year-old man in a wheelchair to leave the inside lane of the M4 motorway.
He was being pushed by his 65-year-old son.
Guardian, 5.6.69

Great Pretender

Returning to his car, a motorist found its bodywork severely dented and the following note tucked behind his windscreen wiper:

"I have just run into your car. People have seen me and are watching me write this. They think I am giving you my name and address. They are wrong."

New York Herald Tribune

If the Name's Fitt. . .

After spending three years and over £2,500 in constructing his dream car, a natty two-seater decorated with 40 feet of chrome trim, Mr James Fitt of Stockport, Lancashire decided to give it a spin.

Ten miles from his do-it-yourself design shop the front inside wheel spun off and struck a milk float.

As Mr Fitt was doing no more than 5 mph at the time of the incident, no harm was done.

Having replaced the wheel and registered a further two miles on the clock, the same wheel left the main body of the vehicle.

Mr Fitt dismounted, retrieved the wheel, carried it back to the car and threw it straight at the windscreen.

Thereafter he tore the seating to shreds, smashed the instrument panel to pieces with the jack and, when four passers-by tried to restrain him, he managed to persuade them to help him with the job.

Mr George Cobb, a house-painter from Salford, said: "It took us a good half-hour to demolish the car completely. We had it strewn all over the road. About 50 people stood about watching us."

Mr Fitt said: "I don't know what happened. I just went berserk."

He was fined £12 for disturbing the peace, and £125 for clearing-up costs.

Anon

Bicycle Made For Four

Mr Dennis Bowler of Revesby, Lincolnshire
was fined £1 for having four on a bike — one on
the handlebars, one on the crossbar, one standing
on the saddle balancing against himself and pedalling
— all three his children who had missed their
school taxi.
Lincolnshire Standard, 27.2.70

U.rinary F.O.

"I was having a shave when there was a loud swishing noise followed by a great thud," said Mr Chris Elkins of Addlestone, Surrey.

"My wife and I went into the garden and saw that our lawn had been seriously dented by a massive lump of ice that had fallen out of the skies."

After some time the police arrived, took it away and stored it in their refrigerator until someone realised that it was a block of frozen urine jettisoned from a passing aircraft.

"What with the number of aircraft about," said a police spokesman, "we are very lucky it wasn't something worse."
Surrey Herald, 10.9.71

To Heaven, via Paradise

The last wish of Miss Foley of Boston, Mass. was to be buried 4,000 miles away on the Isle of Arran.

The burial trip was organised by an undertaker named Sheehan. The fee was £300, door-to-door.

Being a son of Cork, undertaker Sheehan knew that Arran was a desolate and barren hunk of rock, approachable only by rowing-boat. It was therefore arranged that the remains should travel to Shannon by jet, and thereafter by helicopter to Arran.

The coffin was due to arrive in time for eleven o'clock mass on Sunday morning.

Soon after touchdown at Shannon the fine American coffin was crated and attached by means of slings to the helicopter. The journey should have taken no more than twenty minutes.

However, a few minutes after take-off something went wrong; the coffin and the remains of Miss Foley fell four hundred feet into the village of Paradise.

Some hours later the wreckage was collected by van, the remains were transferred to an Irish coffin and at 10.30 on Monday morning they took to the air again from Lahinch Golf Club car park.

Prior to take-off rigorous tests had been applied to the helicopter and its lifting device.

"We did everything except loop the loop," said Mr Emby, a director of Trans World Helicopters. "We are licensed to carry all kinds of freight."

Undertaker Sheehan was enjoying his lunch in a Lahinch hotel when they brought him the news of a second disaster.

The helicopter's pilot had dropped the coffin into the sea off the cliffs of Moher.

At once a search was organised. The Kilronan lifeboat was contacted, but the crew refused to put to sea because no life was at stake.

Said Father McNamara, "No exception can be made in this case."

No such qualms beset Mr Peter Hall, the helicopter's navigator. In order to help a Galway trawler pinpoint the spot where the coffin was last seen floating, he dropped into the sea. "I was in the sea for ten minutes," he said. "It was freezing. There was no sign of the coffin."

Underwater television cameras, skin-divers, spotter planes and the Galway fishing fleet all failed to trace the coffin.

"We thought we had it once," said a frogman, "but it turned out to be a dead sheep."

Anon

On the Spot M.O.T.

Arrested by Garda Collony while driving a 17-year-old mini-car, Mr Rooney explained that he was only driving the uninsured vehicle because he had broken his leg while trying to jack it up, and had failed to get a lift to the hospital.

Said Garda Collony: "I heard the car from about a mile away. At first I thought it was a bomb going off. I approached the vehicle which was going at about five miles an hour and ordered the driver to stop.

"On examination I found that it would not engage in any gear but first, had four completely bald tyres, neither hand nor foot brake worked, the steering was marshy, the battery flat, the spare tyre deflated, three hub-caps missing, the car had no driving mirror and was covered in mud. While I was making my examination the exhaust pipe fell off and the engine boiled over. Mr Rooney was, however, very co-operative."

Mr Rooney explained that he had bought the car "from a passer-by" for £6.00. His wife thought they might sell it to the Beaulieu Car Museum.

Dundalk Democrat, 9.12.72

Tusk! Tusk!

While passing Olympia, the Earl of Dalkeith's aunt got stuck in a traffic jam.

Irritated by exhaust fumes an elephant standing directly in front of her vehicle relieved itself over the bonnet.

Daily Telegraph

Faulty Examiner

A man taking his driving test on a scooter was given the usual instructions to drive over a given route during which time he would be observed and, at one point, the examiner would step out in front of his machine to check his braking reactions.

Three times the man circled the route and saw no sign of his examiner. Finally he returned to the test centre and asked for him.

"We are sorry," he was told. "He stepped in front of the wrong scooter."

West London Observer, 2.9.65

Burial Grounds

Supporting the rejection of Bridport Rural Council's application to build 12 old people's cottages near Tompton, Mr Jack Snaith said: "There is nowhere to park the hearses."

Hampshire Chronicle, 21.11.75

TRAVEL

Strangers on a Train

A scientist was going to a conference by train. The conference — due to last a week — necessitated a journey of two days; during this time he shared a carriage with a woman who looked about 26 but was, as he discovered, 31.

By the time they arrived he knew she was widowed, had a daughter of seven, and was responsible for editing the lay prose issued by a famous Institute.

On the evening of the seventh day the scientist was driven to the station.

His carriage was empty save for the woman who had journeyed down with him. For the best part of a minute they stared at each other in silence. Then, apropos of nothing, he said:

"My name is Ozymandias, king of kings:
Look on my works, ye Mighty, and despair!"
The woman fainted.

When she came round she said: "Those were my husband's two favourite lines of poetry."
The Times

Deep-Frozen Kentucky Chicken

Mr Leonard Moore, a hairdresser's assistant from Olive, Kentucky, abandoned his attempt to row the Bering Straits in a bath after it became icebound two miles off the coast of Little Diomede Island.

"I took four gallons of peanut butter along," he said, "but on the morning of the fifth day it had gone solid. By late afternoon, although the sun was still high, the sea went rather thick. Next morning I was frozen in."

Mr Moore walked ashore.

Daily Mail, 10.7.73

Pee-shooter Misfired

Seeking a place for a quiet piss, Mr William Bertrand nipped over a wall and dropped into Niagara Falls.

A hospital spokesman described his condition as "fair".

Guardian, 5.7.70

Flying Scotsman

To celebrate his 700th drop, Flight Sergeant Hector Macmillan, a parachute instructor, jumped in full Scottish dress while playing *The Road To The Isles* on his bagpipes.
Daily Express

Too Much Rope

Mr Peter Wing (82) and his brother James (79), both of Macaskie, Ontario, returned to their room in the Snaybourne Hotel, Paddington after a day spent seeing the sights.

"We lay down on our beds," said Mr James Wing, "and then we noticed that there was a corpse lying in the corner by the wash-basin. Naturally we called the police."

A police spokesman said that no corpse had been found. However, the brothers admitted that they had been smoking powdered rope.

"We bought it as cannabis in Piccadilly Circus," said Mr Peter Wing. "It is our first holiday abroad and we thought we would give it a try."

Dismissing the charge against the brothers, the magistrate said the effect of smoking powdered rope was extraordinary.

Anon

Pilgrims' Progress

In October 1965 a man and a woman, both wearing tattered overcoats, made their way along the Wandsford stretch of the A1 carrying some twenty parcels.

They did not carry the parcels in two clumps; rather, they placed each parcel on the road and then relayed them forwards one by one, progressing about 100 yards on each move. Having completed one full relay they began all over again, thus making their way north.

They would not give their names. However, to those who spoke to them, the woman said: "We have been on the road for months; always travelling like this with these parcels filled with bits and pieces gathered on the way. We want to see the true England and meet the people. We have a long way to go yet."

Daily Mail, 29.10.65

Religious Training

Travellers on the 3.20 non-stop express from Newcastle to London were surprised when, having assured a fellow passenger that they would not be stopping at York, the Reverend Robert Middlemiss fell onto his knees and began to pray for the train to slow down.

Their surprise turned to amazement when it did and, after apologising to them for any inconvenience caused, the Rev. Middlemiss opened the carriage door and jumped out.

"I was booked to address the British Sailors' Society in York," said Vicar Middlemiss. "I did not want to be late. I am a firm believer in the power of prayer."

A spokesman for British Rail said that Rev. Middlemiss had contravened a bye-law.
Daily Express, 26.9.72

Russian to Buy

Arrested for indecent exposure in the middle of Lenin Square, Kiev, Mr Brian Dicer, a member of the Welsh International football team, said that he had never seen such a happy crowd as the 82,000 who packed the Kiev 'Gagor' stadium.

Walking about the city on the day after the match, Mr Dicer said, "was a real eye-opener. People rushed up and offered to buy the things I had on for fantastic sums. My tie went for a fiver. I got £45 for my jacket, and £30 for my trousers. Before I knew what was happening I was down to my pants and socks."

Mr Dicer told the police that the man to whom he had sold his trousers had assured him that he could buy another pair just round the corner at a quarter of the price, "but when I got to the shop it was closed."

Irish Press, 21.5.75

John Brown's Body...

Mr John Brown and Miss Doreen Wright began their much-discussed journey around the world from Ipswich. The friends envisaged driving to Cape Town in a twenty-year-old van, sailing to Perth and driving back up to Ipswich via Kabul.

However, in Ruanda they were stoned by loyal tribesmen. In Mozambique they were ambushed by patriots. They almost died of thirst in the Kalahari Desert ("where we went as an interesting detour"). Then, when they reached Kimberley, John caught a rare tropical blood disease and died.

Back in Ipswich, Doreen said: "I have come to the conclusion that the people who said we were mad to undertake such a journey were right."

Guardian, 7.7.73

Flight of Fancy

Dazed by his flight from Sydney to London, Mr James Hargreaves accepted the embraces of Mrs Georgina Thorpe, her sister Mrs Arthur Jones, and the vigorous handshake of Mr Arthur Jones.

Led to their car and given the front seat, Mr Hargreaves "took a short after-flight nap", and woke up "in an M1 lay-by".

"He looked like George, he walked like George and he talked like George," said Mrs Thorpe, "but he was not George" — her brother — "who went to Australia ten years ago".

"We stopped for tea in a lay-by after we picked him up," said Mrs Jones. "When we got him into the car I asked the girls if they were absolutely sure that he was their George, as he had been drinking.

"We were in the middle of tea when he woke up, hit me on the nose, leapt out of the car and ran away over the fields, shouting: "Take my money but spare my life!"

Mr Robert Pinner, a farmer, said that he saw Mr Hargreaves hiding behind an electric plough. When he spoke to him, Mr Hargreaves said that he had been kidnapped.

Southend Standard, 24.9.75